Learning iOS Forensics

A practical hands-on guide to acquire and analyze iOS
devices with the latest forensic techniques and tools

Mattia Epifani

Pasquale Stirparo

PUBLISHING

BIRMINGHAM - MUMBAI

Learning iOS Forensics

First published: March 2015

Production reference: 1030315

Published by Packt Publishing Ltd.
Livery Place
35 Livery Street
Birmingham B3 2PB, UK.

ISBN 978-1-78355-351-8

www.packtpub.com

Credits

Authors
Mattia Epifani

Pasquale Stirparo

Reviewers
John B. Baird

Florian Pradines

Lavneet Sharma

Michael Yasumoto

Commissioning Editor
Ashwin Nair

Acquisition Editor
Sonali Vernekar

Content Development Editor
Pooja Nair

Technical Editors
Rosmy George

Novina Kewalramani

Edwin Moses

Copy Editors
Brinda S. Madhu

Vikrant Phadke

Project Coordinator
Leena Purkait

Proofreaders
Simran Bhogal

Maria Gould

Paul Hindle

Clyde Jenkins

Indexer
Monica Ajmera Mehta

Production Coordinator
Nilesh R. Mohite

Cover Work
Nilesh R. Mohite

About the Author

Mattia Epifani (`@mattiaep`) is the CEO at Reality Net–System Solutions, an Italian consulting company involved in InfoSec and digital forensics. He works as a digital forensics analyst for judges, prosecutors, lawyers, and private companies. He is a court witness and digital forensics expert.

He obtained a university degree in computer science in Genoa, Italy, and a master's degree in computer forensics and digital investigations in Milan. Over the last few years, he obtained several certifications in digital forensics and ethical hacking (GCFA, GREM, GMOB, CIFI, CEH, CHFI, ACE, AME, ECCE, CCE, and MPSC) and attended several SANS classes (computer forensics and incident response, Windows memory forensics, mobile device security and ethical hacking, reverse engineering malware, and network forensics analysis).

He speaks regularly on digital forensics in different Italian and European universities (Genova, Milano, Roma, Bolzano, Pescara, Salerno, Campobasso, Camerino, Pavia, Savona, Catania, Lugano, Como, and Modena e Reggio Emilia) and events (Security Summit, IISFA Forum, SANS European Digital Forensics Summit, Cybercrime Conference Sibiu, Athens Cybercrime Conference, and DFA Open Day). He is a member of CLUSIT, DFA, IISFA, ONIF, and Tech and Law Center and the author of various articles on scientific publications about digital forensics. More information is available on his LinkedIn profile (`http://www.linkedin.com/in/mattiaepifani`).

Acknowledgments

My first thank you goes to Pasquale Stirparo. We met in 2009 during a course on digital investigations at the University of Milan. Since then, we became great friends, both with a common passion for digital forensics and the mobile world. This book is the outcome of our continuous discussions on the subject and the exchange of knowledge and opinions. Thank you, Pas! It's always nice working with you!

We, the authors, would like to thank Marco Carlo Spada and Paolo Dal Checco, for their valuable help in revising the entire book and their useful suggestions to improve the final result.

I also want to thank Marco Scarito and Francesco Picasso, my colleagues and friends. Without their daily efforts and our continuous exchange of knowledge, this book would not have been written. I also want to thank my parents, Roberta and Mario, and their (and also mine!) dogs, Nina and Sissi, for supporting me every day!

Then, I would like to thank all the mentors I've had over the years: Giovanni Ziccardi, Gerardo Costabile, Rob Lee, Raul Siles, Jess Garcia, Alessandro Borra, and Alberto Diaspro. Also, a big thank you to my friends and colleagues: Giuseppe Vaciago, Litiano Piccin, Davide Gabrini, Davide D'Agostino, Stefano Fratepietro, Paolo Dal Checco, Andrea Ghirardini, Francesca Bosco, Daniela Quetti, Valerio Vertua, Andrey Belenko, and Vladimir Katalov. Without learning from these teachers and exchanging information with my colleagues, there is not a chance I would be doing what I do today. It is because of them and others who I may not have listed here that I feel proud to pass my knowledge on to those willing to learn.

About the Author

Pasquale Stirparo (@pstirparo) is currently working as a Senior Information Security and Incident Response Engineer at a Fortune 500 company. Prior to this, he founded SefirTech, an Italian company focusing on mobile security, digital forensics, and incident response. Pasquale has also worked at the Joint Research Centre (JRC) of European Commission as a digital forensics and mobile security researcher, focusing mainly on security and privacy issues related to mobile devices communication protocols, mobile applications, mobile malware, and cybercrime. He was also involved in the standardization of digital forensics as a contributor (the first from Italy) to the development of the standard *ISO/IEC 27037: Guidelines for identification, collection and/or acquisition and preservation of digital evidence*, for which he led the WG ISO27037 for the Italian National Body in 2010.

The author of many scientific publications, Pasquale has also been a speaker at several national and international conferences and seminars on digital forensics and a lecturer on the same subject for Polytechnic of Milano and United Nations (UNICRI). Pasquale is a Ph.D candidate at Royal Institute of Technology (KTH), Stockholm. He holds an MSc in computer engineering from Polytechnic of Torino, and he has GCFA, GREM, OPST, OWSE, and ECCE certifications and is a member of DFA, Tech and Law Center, and ONIF. You can find his details on LinkedIn at https://www.linkedin.com/in/pasqualestirparo.

Acknowledgments

This book would have hardly been possible without my great friend Mattia Epifani, who agreed to join me in this incredible journey. Our teamwork and brainstorming sessions, along with his knowledge and advice, have been invaluable. Thank you!

We, the authors, would like to thank Marco Carlo Spada and Paolo Dal Checco, for their valuable help in revising the entire book and their useful suggestions to improve the final result.

I would like to thank my girlfriend, Silvia, for her patience during my many sleepless nights spent on writing and researching. Her continuous encouragement and love have been a source of strength and motivation for me. I am also very grateful to my friends and colleagues, Marco Scarito and Francesco Picasso, for all the years we have spent growing together in this amazing field and for the continual exchange of thoughts and ideas. Finally, a big thank you to my parents, Francesco and Silvia, my sisters, Stella and Carmen, and my brother, Rocco, for their endless support throughout my life.

I also owe a thank you to Maurizio Agazzini, Marco Ivaldi, and Andrea Ghirardini, the very first people who taught me everything when I was just a "kid out of university." They made me fall in love with this field of work. Another thank you goes to Francesca Bosco and Giuseppe Vaciago for putting their trust in me since the very beginning and for their guidance throughout these years. Thanks to my friends and colleagues Paolo Dal Checco, Stefano Fratepietro, Daniela Quetti, and Valerio Vertua as well. Last but not least, a huge thank you goes to Heather Mahalik, Lenny Zeltser, and Raul Siles for being great instructors and sources of inspiration and the whole SANS family and the DFIR community, where the knowledge and passion of great-minded and extraordinary people come together. Thank you!

About the Reviewers

John B. Baird was born on January 2, 1981, and grew up on Anna Maria Island, Florida, United States. He learned about computers and technology himself at the age of 13. In 2004, he started his own technology consulting business. In that role, he provided services and training for residential and business clients in the Tampa Bay Area. Some of his most prominent clients and contractual assignments included AOL, Wells Fargo, and Comcast.

John soon decided to amplify his skill set and take on a more challenging endeavor. Working with computer forensic suites, such as EnCase and FTK, and practicing skills ranging from evidence preservation to interim report writing, he graduated from ITT Technical Institute online as an associate of applied science in computer forensics in December, 2012. He graduated with a summa cum laude honor, scoring 3.8 out of 4.0 GPA, and was awarded sponsorship for National Technical Honor Society in 2012.

John is trying to make a difference in cyber security and is seeking to work hard for an organization, local or across America, to help him meet his goals. He always looks for interesting, new topics to help others, work or to volunteer. His computer forensics portfolio is available at www.johnBbaird.com.

Florian Pradines is a French student in an engineering school, with experience in the information security field. He began programming some websites at the age of 14 and was soon interested in IT security.

Since 2012, he has been working as an IT security consultant for a French company called Phonesec. At the time of writing this book, he has started carrying out professional security audits for some companies on various platforms such as iOS, Android, and websites.

Since 2013, he has been an active member of Open Web Application Security Project (OWASP) where he writes and maintains some tools to help penetration testers conduct their security audits more quickly.

Lavneet Sharma (cipherux) is an entrepreneur working as a CEO in his own data mining start-up known as Corouter Solutions. He has worked as a digital forensics analyst in one of the leading cybercrime investigation companies in India. He is particularly interested in taking advantage of emerging technologies, such as cloud computing and big data analysis, and basic programming technologies, such as Java and Python, to explore and generate new opportunities in the field of information technology. Other than data mining, his fields of interest include cryptography and digital forensics.

He has recently worked on a few commercial (freeware) cryptography tools, both symmetric and asymmetric, to securely sync data across the cloud. He has also developed a high-speed, scalable, and extensible web crawler to run over the cloud in Java.

I would like to sincerely thank the author of this book for giving me a chance to work with a lot of interesting and useful information. I would also like to thank my parents for trusting me and helping me achieve my targets. I would also like to thank my friends for encouraging me to review such a great book and explore such awesome technology.

Michael Yasumoto is a senior forensic examiner with Deadbolt Forensics, a leading provider of computer and mobile forensic services. He is based in Portland, Oregon. In this role, Michael has conducted examinations on a wide variety of computers and mobile devices running on many types of operating systems.

Michael holds a bachelor's degree in chemistry from the University of Washington and a master's degree in computer science from George Washington University. Some of his forensic credentials include Certified Computer Examiner (CCE), EnCase Certified Examiner (EnCE), AccessData Certified Examiner (ACE), Cellebrite Certified Mobile Examiner (CCME), and AccessData Mobile Examiner (AME).

www.PacktPub.com

Support files, eBooks, discount offers, and more

For support files and downloads related to your book, please visit www.PacktPub.com.

Did you know that Packt offers eBook versions of every book published, with PDF and ePub files available? You can upgrade to the eBook version at www.PacktPub.com and as a print book customer, you are entitled to a discount on the eBook copy. Get in touch with us at service@packtpub.com for more details.

At www.PacktPub.com, you can also read a collection of free technical articles, sign up for a range of free newsletters and receive exclusive discounts and offers on Packt books and eBooks.

https://www2.packtpub.com/books/subscription/packtlib

Do you need instant solutions to your IT questions? PacktLib is Packt's online digital book library. Here, you can search, access, and read Packt's entire library of books.

Why subscribe?

- Fully searchable across every book published by Packt
- Copy and paste, print, and bookmark content
- On demand and accessible via a web browser

Free access for Packt account holders

If you have an account with Packt at www.PacktPub.com, you can use this to access PacktLib today and view 9 entirely free books. Simply use your login credentials for immediate access.

Table of Contents

Preface	**1**
Chapter 1: Digital and Mobile Forensics	**7**
Digital forensics	**7**
Mobile forensics	**8**
Digital evidence	**9**
Identification, collection, and preservation of evidence	**11**
Chain of custody	14
Going operational – from acquisition to reporting	**16**
Evidence integrity	17
SIM cards	**18**
SIM security	21
Summary	**21**
Self-test questions	**22**
Chapter 2: Introduction to iOS Devices	**23**
iOS devices	**23**
iPhone	23
iPhone (first model)	24
iPhone 3G	24
iPhone 3GS	24
iPhone 4	25
iPhone 4s	25
iPhone 5	25
iPhone 5c	26
iPhone 5s	26
iPhone 6	26
iPhone 6 Plus	26
iPad	27
iPad (first model)	27
iPad 2	27
iPad 3 (the new iPad)	28

iPad 4 (with Retina display)   28
iPad Air   28
iPad mini   28
iPad mini second generation   29
iPad mini third generation   29
iPod touch   29
iPod touch (first model)   29
iPod touch (second generation)   30
iPod touch (third generation)   30
iPod touch (fourth generation)   30
iPod touch (fifth generation)   30

iOS devices matrix   **30**
iOS operating system   **31**
iDevice identification   **32**
iOS file system   **34**
The HFS+ file system   35
Device partitions   40
System partition   41
Data partition   42
The property list file   44
SQLite database   45
Summary   **46**
Self-test questions   **46**

Chapter 3: Evidence Acquisition from iDevices   **49**
iOS boot process and operating modes   **49**
iOS data security   **50**
Hardware security features   50
File data protection   51
Unique device identifier   **52**
Case study – UDID calculation on iPhone 4s   52
Lockdown certificate   **55**
Search and seizure   **56**
iOS device acquisition   **57**
Direct acquisition   58
Backup or logical acquisition   59
Acquisition with iTunes backup   59
Logical acquisition with forensic tools   60
Case study – logical acquisition with Oxygen Forensic® Suite   61
Advanced logical acquisition   66
Case study – advanced logical acquisition with UFED Physical Analyzer   66
Physical acquisition with forensic tools   69
Case study – physical acquisition with UFED Physical Analyzer   70

The iOS device jailbreaking   **75**
Case study – jailbreaking and physical acquisition with
Elcomsoft iOS Forensic Toolkit   76
Apple support for law enforcement   **78**
Search and seizure flowchart   **79**
Extraction flowchart   **80**
Summary   **82**
Self-test questions   **83**
Chapter 4: Analyzing iOS Devices   **85**
How data are stored   **85**
Timestamps   88
Databases   89
The property list files   89
The iOS configuration files   **89**
Native iOS apps   **91**
Address book   91
Audio recordings   91
Calendar   92
Call history   93
E-mail   94
Images   95
Maps   96
Notes   96
Safari   97
SMS/iMessage   98
Voicemail   98
Other iOS forensics traces   **99**
Clipboard   99
Keyboard   99
Location   100
Snapshots   101
Spotlight   102
Wallpaper   102
Third-party application analysis   **102**
Skype   102
WhatsApp   105
Facebook   107
Cloud storage applications   108
Deleted data recovery   **111**
File carving – is it feasible?   111
Carving SQLite deleted records   112

Case study – iOS analysis with Oxygen Forensics Suite 2014	**112**
Summary	**117**
Self-test questions	**117**
Chapter 5: Evidence Acquisition and Analysis from iTunes Backup	**119**
iTunes backup	**119**
iTunes backup folders	120
iTunes backup content	120
iTunes backup structure	**122**
Standard backup files	123
iTunes backup data extraction	**127**
Case study – iTunes backup analysis with iPBA	127
Encrypted iTunes backup cracking	**130**
Case study – iTunes encrypted backup cracking with EPPB	131
Summary	**136**
Self-test questions	**136**
Chapter 6: Evidence Acquisition and Analysis from iCloud	**139**
iCloud	**139**
iDevice backup on iCloud	**140**
iDevice backup acquisition	**141**
Case study – iDevice backup acquisition and EPPB with usernames and passwords	141
Case study – iDevice backup acquisition and EPPB with authentication token	145
Case study – iDevice backup acquisition with iLoot	148
iCloud Control Panel artifacts on the computer	**149**
Summary	**150**
Self-test questions	**151**
Chapter 7: Applications and Malware Analysis	**153**
Setting up the environment	**153**
The class-dump-z tool	155
Keychain Dumper	156
dumpDecrypted	158
Application analysis	**158**
Data at rest	159
Data in use	159
Data in transit	159
Automating the analysis	**162**
The iOS Reverse Engineering Toolkit	162
idb	165

Summary   **169**
Self-test questions   **170**
Appendix A: References   **171**
Publications freely available   **171**
Tools, manuals, and reports   **172**
Apple's official documentation   **173**
Device security and data protection   **174**
Device hardening   **175**
iTunes backup   **175**
iCloud Backup   **176**
Application data analysis   **176**
Related books   **178**
Appendix B: Tools for iOS Forensics   **181**
Acquisition tools   **181**
iDevice browsing tools and other nonforensic tools   **182**
iDevice backup analyzer   **182**
iDevice encrypted backup   **183**
iCloud Backup   **184**
Jailbreaking tools   **184**
iOS 8   184
iOS 7   184
iOS 6   184
Data analysis   **185**
Forensic toolkit   185
SQLite viewer   185
SQLite record carver   185
Plist viewer   186
iOS analysis suite   186
App analysis tools   186
Consolidated.db   187
App reverse engineering tools   187
Appendix C: Self-test Answers   **189**
Index   **191**

Preface

This book is a complete discussion of state-of-the-art technology used in identification, acquisition, and forensic analysis of mobile devices with the iOS operating system. It is a practical guide that will help investigators understand how to manage scenarios efficiently during their daily work on this type of mobile devices.

The need for a practical guide in this area arises from the growing popularity of iOS devices and the different scenarios that an investigator may face, according to the type of device, the version of the operating system, and the presence or absence of security systems (code lock, backup password, and so on).

The book is divided (conceptually) into four areas. The first part deals with the basic concepts related to methods and guidelines to be followed in the treatment of digital evidence and information specific to an iOS device. The second part covers the basic techniques and tools for acquisition and analysis of an iOS device. The third part goes deep into the methods of extracting data when you do not have the physical device available, which means you need to depend on backup and iCloud. Finally, the fourth part provides an overview of issues related to the analysis of iOS applications and malware.

For those who are new to this field, we recommend a sequential reading of the book, since the arguments are processed in the order of the main phases of a forensic investigation (identification, acquisition, and analysis). For the more experienced readers, and for those who routinely deal with this type of devices, the book can be considered as a useful tool to evaluate different techniques, depending on the type of case that you have to handle.

What this book covers

Chapter 1, Digital and Mobile Forensics, is an introduction to the most important concepts and definitions in the field of digital and mobile forensics, and the life cycle of the digital evidence, which includes identification, acquisition, analysis, and reporting.

Chapter 2, Introduction to iOS Devices, contains useful information and references that will help you learn how to identify the various types of devices (such as iPhone, iPad, and iPod Touch) with respect to their model and iOS version. It also contains basic information about the filesystem used on a specific kind of device.

Chapter 3, Evidence Acquisition from iDevices, explains how to acquire data from iOS devices with respect to their model and iOS version, which was introduced in the previous chapter. Physical, logical, and advanced logical acquisitions are discussed, along with the most useful techniques on how to crack or bypass the passcode set by the user. This chapter presents examples of acquisitions realized with various tools, and provides a useful flow chart before dealing with the acquisition stage.

Chapter 4, Analyzing iOS Devices, provides a complete set of information on how to analyze data stored in the acquired device. Both preinstalled (such as address book, call history, SMS, MMS, and Safari) and third-party applications (such as chat, social network, and cloud storage) are explained, with particular attention to the core artifacts and how to search and recover them.

Chapter 5, Evidence Acquisition and Analysis from iTunes Backup, gives an overview on how to deal with the analysis of an iTunes backup taken from a PC or a Mac, focusing on how to read its content and how to try to attack a protected password set by the user. This chapter also explains how to recover passwords stored in the device when the backup is not protected by a password of its own or when the analyst is able to crack it.

Chapter 6, Evidence Acquisition and Analysis from iCloud, deals with the case in which the owner is using iCloud to store the device backup. You will learn how to recover the credentials or the authorization token useful to retrieve the information stored in Apple servers.

Chapter 7, Applications and Malware Analysis, is an introduction to the core concepts and tools used to perform an application assessment from a security point of view. You will also learn how to deal with mobile malware that may be present on jailbroken devices.

Appendix A, References, is a complete set of references that will help you understand some core concepts explained in the book so that you can go deeper into specific topics.

Appendix B, Tools for iOS Forensics, is a comprehensive collection of open source, freeware, and commercial tools used to acquire and analyze the content of iOS devices.

Appendix C, Self-test Answers, contains the answers to the questions asked in the chapters of the book.

Appendix D, iOS 8 – What It Changes for Forensic Investigators, is an add-on covering the recent news and challenges introduced by the latest version of iOS available at the time of writing this book. This is not present in the book but is available as an online chapter at `https://www.packtpub.com/sites/default/files/downloads/3815OS_Appendix.pdf`.

What you need for this book

This book is designed to allow you to use different operating platforms (Windows, Mac, and Linux) through freeware, open source software, and commercial software. Many of the examples shown can be replicated using either the software tested by the authors or equivalent solutions that have been mentioned in *Appendix B, Tools for iOS Forensics*. Some specific cases require the use of commercial platforms, and among those, we preferred the platforms that we use in our daily work as forensic analysts (such as Cellebrite UFED, Oxygen Forensics, Elcomsoft iOS Forensic Toolkit, and Elcomsoft Phone Breaker). In any case, we were inspired by the principles of ease of use, completeness of information extracted, and the correctness of the presentation of the results by the software. This book is not meant to be a form of advertising for the aforementioned software in any way, and we encourage you to repeat the tests carried out on one operating platform on other platforms and software applications as well.

Who this book is for

This book is intended mainly for a technical audience, and more specifically for forensic analysts (or digital investigators) who need to acquire and analyze information from mobile devices running iOS. This book is also useful for computer security experts and penetration testers because it addresses some issues that must be definitely taken into consideration before the deployment of this type of mobile devices in business environments or situations where data security is a necessary condition. Finally, this book can be also of interest to developers of mobile applications, and they can learn what data is stored in these devices where the application is used. Thus, they will be able to improve security.

Conventions

In this book, you will find a number of styles of text that distinguish among different kinds of information. Here are some examples of these styles, and explanations of their meanings.

Code words in text, database table names, folder names, filenames, file extensions, pathnames, dummy URLs, user input, and Twitter handles are shown as follows: "Compile the source file by simply typing the `make` command."

A URL is written as follows:

`http://www.sqlite.org/`

A pathname is written as follows:

`/private/var/root/Library/Lockdown/data_ark.plist`

Any command-line input or output is written as follows:

```
$ iproxy 2222 22
$ ssh usb
```

New terms and **important words** are shown in bold. Words that you see on the screen, in menus or dialog boxes for example, appear in the text like this: "The first popup appears on the computer in iTunes and it requests the user to click on **Continue**."

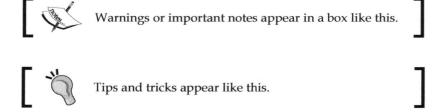

Warnings or important notes appear in a box like this.

Tips and tricks appear like this.

Reader feedback

Feedback from our readers is always welcome. Let us know what you think about this book—what you liked or may have disliked. Reader feedback is important for us to develop titles that you really get the most out of.

To send us general feedback, simply send an e-mail to `feedback@packtpub.com`, and mention the book title via the subject of your message.

If there is a topic that you have expertise in and you are interested in either writing or contributing to a book, see our author guide on `www.packtpub.com/authors`.

Customer support

Now that you are the proud owner of a Packt book, we have a number of things to help you to get the most from your purchase.

Downloading the color images of this book

We also provide you with a PDF file that has color images of the screenshots/ diagrams used in this book. The color images will help you better understand the changes in the output. You can download this file from `https://www.packtpub. com/sites/default/files/downloads/3815OS_ColorImages.pdf`.

Errata

Although we have taken every care to ensure the accuracy of our content, mistakes do happen. If you find a mistake in one of our books—maybe a mistake in the text or the code—we would be grateful if you would report this to us. By doing so, you can save other readers from frustration and help us improve subsequent versions of this book. If you find any errata, please report them by visiting `http://www.packtpub.com/ submit-errata`, selecting your book, clicking on the **errata submission form** link, and entering the details of your errata. Once your errata are verified, your submission will be accepted and the errata will be uploaded on our website, or added to any list of existing errata, under the Errata section of that title. Any existing errata can be viewed by selecting your title from `http://www.packtpub.com/support`.

Piracy

Piracy of copyright material on the Internet is an ongoing problem across all media. At Packt, we take the protection of our copyright and licenses very seriously. If you come across any illegal copies of our works, in any form, on the Internet, please provide us with the location address or website name immediately so that we can pursue a remedy.

Please contact us at `copyright@packtpub.com` with a link to the suspected pirated material.

We appreciate your help in protecting our authors, and our ability to bring you valuable content.

Questions

You can contact us at `questions@packtpub.com` if you are having a problem with any aspect of the book, and we will do our best to address it.

1

Digital and Mobile Forensics

In this chapter, we will quickly go through the definition and principles of digital forensics and, more specifically, of mobile forensics. We will understand what digital evidence is and how to properly handle it and, last but not least, we will cover the methodology for the identification and preservation of mobile evidences.

Digital forensics

Not so long ago we would be talking mainly, if not solely, about computer forensics and computer crimes, such as an attacker breaking into a computer network system and stealing data. This would involve two types of offense: unlawful/unauthorized access and data theft. As cellphones became more popular, the new field of mobile forensics developed.

Nowadays, things have changed radically and are still changing at a quite fast pace as the technology evolves. Digital forensics, which includes all disciplines dealing with electronic evidences is also being applied to common crimes, to those that, at least by definition, are not strictly IT crimes. Today more than ever we live in a society that is fully digitalized, and people are equipped with any kind of device, which have different types of capabilities but all of them process, store, and transmit information (mainly over the Internet). This means that forensic investigators have to be able to deal with all these devices.

As defined at the first **Digital Forensics Research Workshop (DFRWS)** in 2001, digital forensics is stated as:

> *"The use of scientifically derived and proven methods toward the preservation, collection, validation, identification, analysis, interpretation, documentation and presentation of digital evidence derived from digital sources for the purpose of facilitating or furthering the reconstruction of events found to be criminal, or helping to anticipate unauthorized actions shown to be disruptive to planned operations."*

As Casey asserted in (*Casey, 2011*):

> *"In this modern age, it is hard to imagine a crime that does not have a digital dimension."*

Criminals of all kinds use technology to facilitate their offenses, to communicate with their peers, to recruit other criminals, to launder money, commit credit card fraud, to gather information on their victims, and so on. This obviously creates new challenges for all the different actors involved such as attorneys, judges, law enforcement agents, as well as forensic examiners.

Among the cases solved in the last years, there were kidnappings where the kidnapper was caught thanks to the request for the ransom sent by e-mail from his mobile phone. There have been many cases of industrial espionage where unfaithful employees were hiding projects in the memory card of their smartphones, cases of drug dealing solved, thanks to evidence found in the backup of mobile phones that were on the computer, and many others. Even the largest robberies of our time are now being conducted via computer networks.

Mobile forensics

Mobile forensics is the digital forensics field of study, focusing on mobile devices. Among the different digital forensics fields, mobile forensics is without doubt the fastest growing and evolving area of study, having an impact on many different situations from corporate to criminal investigations, to intelligence gathering, which is every day higher. Moreover, the importance of mobile forensics is increasing exponentially due to the continuous and fast growth of the mobile market. One of the most interesting peculiarities of mobile forensics is that mobile devices, particularly mobile phones, usually belong to a single individual, while this is not always the case with a computer that may be shared among employees of a company or members of a family. For this reason, their analysis gives access to plenty of personal information.

Mobile devices present many new challenges from a forensics perspective. Additionally, new models of phones are being developed all around the world with new phones being released every week. Such variety of mobile devices makes it difficult, or almost impossible, to develop a single solution, whether a process or a tool, to address all possible scenarios.

Just think of all the applications people have installed in their smartphones: IM clients, web browsers, social networks clients, password managers, navigation systems, and much more, other than the "default" classic ones such as an address book, which can provide a lot more information other than just the phone number for each contact that has been saved. Moreover, syncing such devices with the computer has become a very easy and smooth process, and all user activities, schedules, to-do lists, and everything else is stored inside the smartphone. Isn't that enough to profile a person and reconstruct all their recent activities, other than building the network of contacts?

Finally, in addition to such a variety of smartphones and operating systems such as Apple iOS, Google Android, Blackberry OS, and Microsoft Windows Phone, there is a massive number of so-called "feature phones" using older mobile OS systems.

Therefore, it's pretty clear that when talking about mobile/smartphones forensics, there is so much more than just phone call printouts. In fact, with a complete examination, we can retrieve SMS/MMS, pictures, videos, installed applications, e-mails, geolocation data, and so on, both present and deleted information.

Digital evidence

Other than bringing a whole new series of challenges and complexity, the positive aspect to the increasing use of technology by criminals, and in particular, the involvement of mobile devices, has resulted in a high availability of digital evidence that can be used to track down and prosecute offenders. Moreover, while classical physical evidence may be destroyed, digital evidence, most of the time, leaves several traces.

Over the years, there have been several definitions of what digital evidence actually is, some of them focusing particularly on the evidentiary aspects of proof to be used in court, such as the one proposed by the **Standard Working Group on Digital Evidence (SWGDE)**, stating that:

> *"Digital evidence is any information of probative value that is either stored or transmitted in a digital form."*

The definition proposed by the **International Organization of Computer Evidence (IOCE)** states:

> *"Digital evidence is information stored or transmitted in binary form that may be relied on in court."*

The definition given by E. Casey (Casey, 2000), refers to digital evidence as:

> *"Physical objects that can establish that a crime has been committed, can provide a link between a crime and its victim, or can provide a link between a crime and its perpetrator."*

While all of them are correct, as previously said, all of these definitions focus mostly on proof and tend to disregard data that are simply useful to an investigation.

For this reason and for the purpose of this book, we will refer to the definition given by Carrier in 2006 (Carrier, 2006) where digital evidence is defined as:

> *"Digital data that supports or refutes a hypothesis about digital events or the state of digital data."*

This definition is a more general one, but matches better with the current state of digital evidence and its value within the entire investigation process.

Also from a standardization point of view, there have been, and still are, many attempts to define guidelines and best practices for digital forensics on how to handle digital evidence. Other than several guidelines and special publications from NIST, there is a new standard from ISO/IEC that has been released in 2012, the *ISO 27037 Guidelines for identification, collection and/or acquisition and preservation of digital evidence*, which is not specific to mobile forensics but it's related to digital forensics in general, aiming to build a standard procedure for collecting and handling digital evidence, which will be legally recognized and accepted in court in different countries. This is a really important goal if you consider the "lack of borders" in the Internet era, particularly when it comes to digital crimes where illicit actions can be perpetrated by attackers from anywhere in the world.

Identification, collection, and preservation of evidence

In order to be useful in court, but also during the entire investigation phase, digital evidence must be collected, preserved, and analyzed in a forensically sound manner. This means that each single step, from the identification to the reporting, has to be carefully and strictly followed. Historically, we have used to refer to a methodology as *forensically sound* if and only if it would imply the original source of evidence to remain unmodified and unaltered. This was mostly true when talking about classical computer forensics, in scenarios where the forensic practitioner found the computer switched off or had to deal with external hard drives, although not completely true even in these situations. But since the rise of live forensics, this concept has become more and more untrue. In fact, methods and tools for acquiring memory from live systems inevitably alter, even if just a little bit, the target system where they are run on. The advent of mobile forensics stresses even more this concept, because mobile devices, smartphones in particular, are networked devices, continuously exchanging data through several communication protocols such as GSM/CDMA, Wi-Fi, Bluetooth, and so on. Moreover, in order to make an acquisition of a mobile device, forensic practitioners need to have some degree of interaction with the device. Based on the type, a smartphone can need more or less interaction, altering in this way the "original" state of the device.

All of this does not mean that preservation of the source evidence is useless, but that it is nearly impossible in the mobile field. Therefore, it becomes of extreme importance to thoroughly document every single step taken during the collection, preservation, and acquisition phases. Using this approach, forensic practitioners will be able to demonstrate that they have been as un-intrusive as possible. As stated in (*Casey, 2011*):

> "*One of the keys to forensic soundness is documentation. A solid case is built on supporting documentation that reports on where the evidence originated and how it was handled. From a forensic standpoint, the acquisition process should change the original evidence as little as possible and any changes should be documented and assessed in the context of the final analytical results.*"

When in the presence of mobile devices to be collected, it is good practice for the forensic practitioner to consider the following points:

- Take note of the current location where the device has been found.

- Report the device status (switched on or off, broken screen, and so on).

- Report date, time, and other information visible on the screen in case the device is switched on, for example, by taking a picture of the screen.

- Look very carefully for the presence of memory cards. Although it is not the case of the iOS devices, generally many mobile phones have a slot for an external memory card, where pictures and chat databases are usually stored and many other types of user data.

- Look very carefully for the presence of cables related to the mobile phone that is being collected, especially if you don't have a full set of cables in your lab. Many mobile phones have their own cables to connect to the computer and to recharge the battery.

- Search for the original **Subscriber Identity Module (SIM)** package, because that is where the PIN and **PIN unblocking key (PUK)** codes are written.

- Take pictures of every item before collection.

But modifications in mobile devices can happen not only because of the interaction with the forensic practitioner but also due to interaction with the network, voluntary or not. In fact digital evidence in mobile devices can be lost completely as they are susceptible to being overwritten by new data, for example, the smartphone receiving an SMS while it is being collected, thus overwriting possible evidence previously stored in the same area of memory of the newly arrived SMS, or upon receiving a remote wiping command over a wireless network. Most of today's smartphone and iOS devices can be configured to be completely wiped remotely.

From a real case

While searching inside the house of a person under investigation, law enforcement agents found and seized, among other things, computers and a smartphone. After cataloguing and documenting everything, they put all the material into boxes to bring them back to the barracks. Once back in their laboratory, when taking the smartphone to acquire it in order to proceed with the forensics analysis, they noticed the smartphone was "empty" and like "brand new". The owner had wiped it remotely.

Therefore, isolating the mobile device from all radio networks is a fundamental step in the process of preservation of the evidence. There are several ways to achieve this, all with their own pros and cons, as follows:

- **Airplane mode**: Enabling Airplane mode on a device requires some sort of interaction, which may pose some risks of modification by the forensic practitioner. This is one of the best possible options since it implies that all wireless communication chips are switched off. In this case, it is always good to document the action taken also with pictures and/or videos. Normally, this is possible only if the phone is not password-protected or, in this case, the password is known. However, for iDevices with iOS 7 or higher, it is also possible to enable airplane mode by lifting the dock from the bottom, where there will be a button with the shape of a plane. This is possible only if the **Access on Lock Screen** option is enabled from **Settings | Control Center**.

- **Faraday's bag**: This item is a sort of envelope made of conducting material, which blocks out static electric fields and electromagnetic radiations, completely isolating the device from communicating with external networks. It is based, as the name suggests, on Faraday's law. This is the most common solution, particularly useful when the device is being carried from the crime scene to the lab after the seizure. However, the use of Faraday's bag will make the phone continuously search for a network, which will cause the battery to quickly drain. Unfortunately, it is also risky to plug a power cable outside that will go inside the bag, because this may act as antenna. Moreover, it is important to keep in mind that when you remove it from the bag (once arrived in the lab) the phone will again be exposed to the network, so you would need either a shielded lab environment or a Faraday solution that would allow you to access the phone while it is still inside the shielded container, without the need for external power cables.

- **Jamming**: A jammer is used to prevent a wireless device from communicating by sending out radio waves along the same frequencies of that device. In our case, it would jam the GSM/UMTS/LTE frequencies that mobile phones use to connect with cellular base stations to send/receive data. Beware that this practice may be considered illegal in some countries, since it will also create interferences to any other mobile device in the range of the jammer, disrupting their communications too.

- **Switching off the device**: This is a very risky practice because it may activate authentication mechanisms, such as PIN codes or passcodes that are not available to the forensic practitioner, or encryption mechanisms, with the risk of delaying or even blocking the acquisition of the mobile device.

- **Removing the SIM card**: Although in most mobile devices this operation implies removing the battery and therefore all the risks and consequences we just mentioned regarding switching off the device, in the iOS devices this task is quite straightforward and easy, and it does not imply removing the battery (in iOS devices this is not possible). Moreover, SIMs can have PIN protection enabled; by removing it from the phone it may lock the SIM, preventing its content from being displayed. However, bear in mind that removing the SIM card will isolate the device only from the cellular network while other networks, such as Wi-Fi or Bluetooth, may still be active and therefore need to be addressed.

The preceding image shows a SIM card extracted from an iPhone with just a clip, taken from http://www.maclife.com/.

Chain of custody

Talking about documenting and the preservation of digital evidence, one of the most important steps is the correct and comprehensive compilation of the **chain of custody**. The purpose of this document is twofold: on one hand, to keep record of each person who handled the evidence, enabling the identification of access and movement of potential digital evidence at any given point in time; and on the other hand, to maintain documentation demonstrating that the digital evidence has not been altered since it was collected while passing through the hands of the several analysts listed in the document.

Therefore, some of the information that the chain of custody should contain is as follows:

- A unique evidence identifier
- Who accessed the evidence and the time and location it took place
- Who checked the evidence in and out from the evidence preservation facility and when
- Motivations about why the evidence was checked out
- It must provide the hash value(s) of the evidence in order to prove that it has not been tampered with since it was last assigned to the previous person listed in the chain of custody
- Although the forensics investigation must never be performed directly on the original device/file, this can be done if any unavoidable changes to the potential digital evidence have to be performed and the justification for the introduction of such changes, as well as the name of the individual responsible

The following image shows a sample of chain custody proposed by NIST:

EVIDENCE CHAIN OF CUSTODY TRACKING FORM

Case Number: _____ Offense: _____
Submitting Officer: (Name/ID#) _____
Victim: _____
Suspect: _____
Date/Time Seized: _____ Location of Seizure: _____

Description of Evidence		
Item #	Quantity	Description of Item (Model, Serial #, Condition, Marks, Scratches)

Chain of Custody				
Item #	Date/Time	Released by (Signature & ID#)	Received by (Signature & ID#)	Comments/Location

Going operational – from acquisition to reporting

Especially in mobile forensics, where information visible may be more volatile, but also in classical computer forensics, sometimes there may be the urgency to acquire the data available. Information may vanish before being able to isolate or properly handle the device. In such cases, effective on-scene triage processes and tools may preserve evidence that would otherwise be lost. Such processes may include taking immediate pictures or videos recording the screen of the device before proceeding with any other type of operation.

Having said that, once the mobile device has been handled correctly, forensic practitioners may proceed with the acquisition of the evidence from the device. In mobile forensics, and particularly for iOS devices, there are the following three different types of possible acquisition:

- **Physical**: This is the optimal and most desired option. A physical acquisition consists of an exact "bit-to-bit" copy of the device. This is the most comprehensive option since it also allows you to recover potentially deleted files.

- **File System**: This is the second best option when physical acquisition is not possible for whatever reason. This type of acquisition lets the forensic practitioner extract all the files visible at file system level. In this way, it will be possible to analyze all active files, those that would be visible by browsing the file system, but it will not be possible to recover potentially deleted files.

- **Logical**: With this type of acquisition, it is possible to extract part of the file system. It consists of the data available by performing the backup of the device, via iTunes in the case of iOS devices. Unfortunately, on iOS, a logical/backup acquisition does not extract important files such as e-mails, geolocation databases, the app cache folder, and so on. Although it is the least comprehensive of the three, sometimes this may be the only option available.

The preceding three acquisition methods are the main methods for acquiring an iOS device, we will see more about this in detail later. In the next chapters, we will dive deep into each of the different methodologies, explaining how to behave in every different possible situation and we will see most of the different tools available for performing the acquisition and further analysis of a physical file system and logical acquisition.

Mobile forensics, however, may also include the need to adopt some "offensive security" techniques. Depending on the device model and iOS version, in order to make a physical acquisition we may need to jailbreak the device, hopefully with a tethered technique so that modifications will not be persistent on the device and it will be restored once restarted. Even in cases when we can only perform an untethered jailbreak, such modifications will affect only the iOS device system partition, leaving the user partition unchanged and therefore the evidence preserved.

Another offensive technique we may need to use is password cracking. As we will see later, often we may find ourselves in front of a password-protected device. Also according to the different models and iOS versions, it may be possible to perform brute force attacks at the passcode set by the user.

All of these more "invasive" techniques will need to be fully documented in the final report, detailing methodology, techniques, and tools used. It is very important, especially because of their invasiveness, to know very well the tools and techniques used in order to be able to explain what and where modifications have happened, and why they did not alter the evidence to the point of compromising it. Good reporting is the key.

Evidence integrity

It has been mentioned already multiple times that when handling mobile devices, it is basically always impossible not to interact with the device and therefore alter to some extent its current status. However, this does not mean that in mobile forensics there is no need or reason to put in place mechanisms of evidence integrity. In fact, once the acquisition has been completed, there must be in place some integrity verification mechanism for the data that has been extracted from the mobile device, be it an iTunes backup, a full physical acquisition, or simply a single file. In digital forensics, such a process of verifying the integrity of digital evidence is completed by comparing the digital fingerprint of the evidence taken at the time of acquisition with the digital fingerprint of the evidence in the current state. Such a fingerprint is also known as a **hash value** or **message digest**. Hashing functions are specific one-way mathematic functions such that given any input of arbitrary length, it will produce as result an output of a fixed given length. The same input will always produce the same output. This means that even if a single bit is changed, the new hash value will be completely different. The following table shows how simply by modifying only the case of two characters in the same sentence, the resulted hash value is completely different:

Input value	MD5 output
ios Forensics book	9effa61083b07a164c5471d020fa4306
iOS Forensics book	e6196e1b4f0d1535244eaab534428542

The two most common algorithms used to calculate hash values are MD5 and SHA-1. The MD5 algorithm produces an output value of 128-bit, while the SHA-1 algorithm produces an output of 160-bit. The other important characteristic of this type of algorithms is that it is computationally unfeasible and highly improbable to produce two messages with the same digest, or even less producing a message with a specified target digest. This problem is known as **collision**. Although researchers have found that two files that have the same hash value can be generated for both MD5 and SHA-1, this has been proved only under certain controlled conditions. Fortunately, this type of hash collision does not invalidate the use of MD5 or SHA-1 to document the integrity of digital evidence. Since it is basically impossible to produce two files that have the same MD5 and SHA-1 hash value (or in general two hash values generated by two different independent algorithms), it is a good practice to generate both MD5 and SHA-1 hash values for each piece of digital evidence produced or collected.

SIM cards

When conducting forensic examinations of mobile devices, it is also important to acquire and analyze the contents of associated SIM cards. The SIM is a type of smart card that allows the mobile device to connect to the cellular network through the cryptographic keys embedded in the SIM itself. The SIM is mainly characterized by the following two different codes that can be retrieved:

- **Integrated Circuit Card Identification (ICCID)**: This code is a 20 digit code that internationally and univocally identifies each SIM card

- **International Mobile Subscriber Identity (IMSI)**: This is a unique number 15 digits long (somewhere, like in South Africa, it's 14), which univocally identifies a user inside the mobile network

Although it is not the case with iOS devices, there might be multiple SIM cards that an individual uses within the same device for different purposes, since some mobile devices support functioning with dual SIM cards.

In addition, the storage capacity and utilization of SIM cards has increased a lot and may contain a big amount of relevant information. Just to give you an idea of the amount of data that could be possible to store (or hide) inside a SIM, consider that inside a 128 Kb standard SIM card, it is possible to write up to 17 Kb of data. The whole *United States Declaration of Independence* takes just 11 Kb.

Some of the useful information to recover from a SIM card may be the list of incoming/outgoing phone calls, contacts information, the SMS content, for which it is possible to recover even those that have been deleted, and the location of the last cell to which the device was connected.

Looking into the details of the SIM card (Gubian, 2007), it is possible to see the hierarchical n-ary structure of the file system that has three different kinds of files, with the content of each file defined in the following GSM technical specification (GSM 11.11):

- **3F = Master File (MF)**: Its structure is composed just by a header and it is the root of the file system in the SIM card. Its address, which is the offset for every other file, is 3F00.

- **7F/5F = Dedicated File (DF)**: As for the MF, its structure is composed just by a header plus EFs. A DF can be compared to a normal directory/folder in our PC.

- **2F = Elementary file (EF) under the master file and 6F/4F = Elementary file under a dedicated file**: Its structure is composed by a header plus a body, which represents itself (for example, the SMS).

The following diagram gives an example of this hierarchical structure (the file system structure of a SIM):

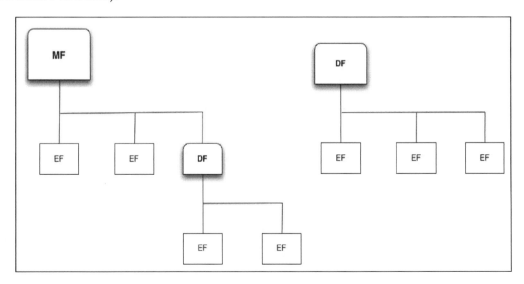

The GSM technical specification already provides some files with common names. Some of the most interesting among the standard ones may be the 3F00:7F10 directory, named DF_TELECOM, which contains service-related information, including user-created data such as SMS and last numbers dialed. The 3F00:7F20 directory, named DF_GSM, contains network-related information for GSM 900 MHz band operation (DF_DCS1800 contains information for 1800 MHz band operation). The ICCID and IMSI mentioned previously can be found at 3F00:2FE2, named EF_ICCID, and 3F00:7F20:6F07, named EFIMSI, respectively. The following table presents some of the well-known information that can be found inside the SIM card and their respective locations:

Description	Location
SMS	7F10:6F3C
MSISDN	7F10:6F40
Last Dialed Numbers (LDN)	7F10:6F44
Abbreviated Dial Numbers (AND)	7F10:6F3A
IMSI	7F10:6F07

In the SIM, the access to each file (EF) is ruled by a certain number of privilege levels, which allow or deny certain actions according to the "role" the user has (which is given from the privilege). Some of the "useful" privileges are ALWays, CHV1, and CHV2. Those are the privileges that allow the owner of the SIM card (or anyway the user who knows the codes) to access and modify the content of such files. For instance, any file that has one of these privileges related to the UPDATE command, allows those that know such codes (CHV1/CHV2) to modify the information inside that file. The following table summarizes the access conditions for the SIM cards:

Level	Access conditions
0	ALWays
1	CHV1
2	CHV2
3	Reserved for GSM future use
4 to 14	ADM
15	NEVer

SIM security

Other than ICCID and IMSI, mainly related to the SIM itself, the other two important codes useful to know (actually, almost indispensable) when conducting an analysis are the PIN code and the PUK code. The PIN code is used to authenticate the user to the system, while the PUK code is used to unlock the SIM card after three incorrect attempts to insert the PIN code. Therefore, brute forcing the PIN is generally ineffective, because three failed PIN attempts will result in the SIM being locked.

Fortunately, the SIM cards have a PUK and many **network service providers (NSP)** can provide, to law enforcements with a proper legal authorization signed by a judge (warrant), the PUK to get around the PIN or to access a locked SIM card.

If an incorrect PUK code is inserted 10 times, the SIM will block itself permanently, making its content completely inaccessible. This is something to keep in mind before starting a brute force guessing against those two codes.

Summary

In this chapter, we gave a general introduction to digital forensics for those relatively new to this area of study and a good recap to those already into the field, keeping the specificity of the mobile forensics field in mind. We have seen what digital evidence is and how it should be handled, presenting several techniques to isolate the mobile device from the network. You should always remember the importance of documenting any action taken (chain of custody, final report, and so on) and to put in place the mechanisms to verify the integrity of the evidence (hash values). We also talked about the different acquisitions techniques for the iOS devices, anticipating some terms and technologies that will be covered in full detail in the next chapters of this book, from A to Z. Last but not least, we talked about the SIM card, how it is structured, and what type of useful information we can expect to find inside.

In the next chapter, we will start focusing purely on the mobile forensics of Apple devices. In particular, you will have an introduction to the iOS devices, OS, and the file system.

Self-test questions

1. What is the best option to isolate a mobile device before acquisition?

    1. Jammer

    2. Faraday's bag

    3. Airplane mode

    4. Switch off the device

2. What is the most comprehensive acquisition method?

    1. Logical

    2. Advanced logical

    3. File system

    4. Physical

3. How is the code that internationally and univocally identifies each SIM card called?

    1. IMSI

    2. ICCID

    3. PUK

    4. GSM

4. How many PUK attempts do we have before the SIM card becomes completely inaccessible?

    1. 3

    2. 5

    3. 10

    4. 15

Introduction to iOS Devices

The purpose of this chapter is to introduce the basic aspects for the forensic analysis of an iOS device. In the first part, the different types and models of the Apple devices are shown, with an indication of the methodologies and techniques to accurately identify the model that you have to acquire. The second part analyzes the fundamental principles of the operating system (types, versions, and so on) and the type and structure of the file system used on these devices.

iOS devices

According to the commonly used definition, an iOS device is a device that uses the iOS operating system. Currently, we have four types of devices: iPhone, iPad, iPad mini, and iPod touch.

iPhone

The most famous iDevice is certainly the iPhone, which has caused a complete revolution in the concept of cellphones, being based on a multi-touch screen, a virtual keyboard, and few physical buttons (the Home, Volume, Power on/off, and Ringer/Vibration buttons).

iPhone (first model)

The first model of the iPhone, known simply as **iPhone**, is equipped with a S5L8900 ARM processor at 620 MHz (underclocked to 412 MHz), 128 MB of RAM, and it uses a cellular connection type quad band GSM/GPRS/EDGE (850/900/1800/1900 MHz), as well as supporting Wi-Fi connectivity 802.11 b/g and Bluetooth 2.0 + EDR (information on how Bluetooth is implemented is available at http://support.apple.com/kb/HT3647). The phone is identified by the model number A1203 and the hardware string iPhone1,1. With regards to the software, it originally used an ancestor of the iOS operating system, known as iPhone OS 1.0. The latest supported version is iPhone OS 3.1.3.

iPhone 3G

The second model produced by Apple, known as **iPhone 3G**, since it added support for the 3G cellular network, is equipped with a S5L8900 ARM processor and 128 MB of RAM. In addition to support for the 3G network (UMTS/HSDPA up to 3.6 Mbit/s at 850, 1900, and 2100 MHz), the main innovation in the hardware was the presence of a GPS chip, which is used for geolocation services. The phone is identified by the model number A1241 (or A1324 for devices sold in China) and the string iPhone1,2. With regards to the software, it originally used iPhone OS 2.0. The latest supported version is iOS 4.2.1.

iPhone 3GS

The third model produced by Apple, known as **iPhone 3GS**, is equipped with a S5L8920 833 MHz ARM processor (underclocked to 600 MHz) and 256 MB of RAM. From the point of view of the forensic analysis, it is interesting to highlight that starting from this model, it is possible to geotag images, making it possible for an investigator to identify the place where a picture was taken. The phone is identified by the model number A1303 (or A1325 for devices sold in China) and the string iPhone2,1. With regards to the software, it originally used iPhone OS 3.0. The latest supported version is iOS 6.1.6. The production of these devices was discontinued in September 2012.

iPhone 4

The fourth model produced by Apple is known as **iPhone 4**. It is a completely renewed device compared to the previous iPhone models, both in appearance and functionality. The device is more squared in its aesthetic form and presents several hardware improvements: an Apple A4 S5L8930 1 GHz processor (underclocked to 800 MHz), 512 MB of RAM, a 5 MP camera with ability to shoot videos in HD (720p), and a 3-axis gyroscope. The phone is identified by three model numbers: A1332 (GSM model) and A1349 (CDMA model) and by three strings iPhone3,1; iPhone3,2; and iPhone3,3. With regards to the software, it originally used iOS 4.0, which is the first version with the new name. The latest supported version is iOS 7.1.2.

iPhone 4s

The fifth model produced by Apple, known as **iPhone 4s**, is aesthetically very similar to iPhone 4, except for the presence of two cuts on the upper part of both sides. The new hardware consists of an Apple A5 S5L8940 1 GHz processor (underclocked to 800 MHz), 512 MB of RAM, support for HSPA+ up to 14.4 Mbit/s, and an 8 MP rear camera with ability to shoot videos in HD (1080p). The phone is identified by the model number A1387 (or A1431 for devices distributed in China) and the string iPhone4,1. With regards to the software, it originally used iOS 5.0. Currently, iPhone 4s is supported by the latest available version (iOS 8.1).

iPhone 5

The sixth model produced by Apple, known as **iPhone 5**, uses an Apple A6 S5L8950 processor 1.3 GHz, 1 GB of RAM, and it supports HSPA+ and LTE cellular networks. It is also equipped with a 1.2 MP front camera for pictures and video up to 720p HD quality. It is the first device in the series with a 4" screen. The phone is identified by three model numbers: A1428 (GSM model), A1429 (GSM and CDMA model), and A1442 (CDMA model for China) and by two strings: iPhone5,1 (USA version with LTE support) and iPhone5,2 (other countries). With regards to the software, it originally used iOS 6.0. Currently, iPhone 5 is supported by the latest available version (iOS 8.1).

iPhone 5c

The seventh model produced by Apple, known as **iPhone 5c**, uses the same processor and the same amount of RAM as the iPhone 5 model, from which it differs in an LTE network support extended to the whole world and a more powerful battery. The phone is identified by five model numbers: A1526 (China), A1532 (North American model), A1456 (the U.S. and Japanese model), A1507 (Europe), and A1529 (Asia and Oceania) and by two strings: iPhone5,3 and iPhone5,4. With regards to the software, it originally used iOS 7.0. Currently, iPhone 5c is supported by the latest available version (iOS 8.1).

iPhone 5s

The eighth model produced by Apple, known as **iPhone 5s**, uses an Apple A7 S5L8960 processor 1.3 GHz, 1 GB of RAM, and the biometric authentication system based on fingerprints, called Touch-ID. It also has a motion coprocessor Apple M7. The phone is identified by five model numbers: A1528 (China), A1533 (North American model), A1453 (the U.S. and Japanese model), A1457 (Europe), and A1530 (Asia and Oceania) and by two strings: iPhone6,1 and iPhone6,2. With regards to the software, it originally used iOS 7.0. Currently, iPhone 5s is supported by the latest available version (iOS 8.1).

iPhone 6

The ninth model produced by Apple, known as **iPhone 6**, uses an Apple A8 APL1011 processor 1.38 GHz with 1 GB of RAM. It has also a motion coprocessor Apple M8. The phone is identified by two model numbers: A1549 (North America) and A1586 (global) and by the string iPhone7,2. With regards to the software, it originally used iOS 8.0. Currently, iPhone 6 is supported by the latest available version (iOS 8.1).

iPhone 6 Plus

The tenth model produced by Apple, known as **iPhone 6 Plus**, uses an Apple A8 APL1011 processor 1.38 GHz with 1 GB of RAM. It has also a motion coprocessor Apple M8. The phone is identified by two model numbers: A1522 (North America) and A1524 (global) and by the string iPhone7,1. With regards to the software, it originally used iOS 8.0. Currently, iPhone 6 Plus is supported by the latest available version (iOS 8.1).

iPad

After the success of the iPhone, Apple carried out the project of designing and producing a larger version, which for the first time gave substance to Steve Jobs' idea in 1983:

> *"Apple's strategy is really simple. What we want to do is we want to put an incredibly great computer in a book that you can carry around with you."*

After the launch of the first iPad, Jobs said that Apple had begun to develop the iPad tablet before iPhone, but that had subsequently decided to concentrate its efforts in the development of iPhone.

iPad (first model)

The first model of iPad, known simply as **iPad** (or **iPad first generation**), is equipped with a 1 GHz S5L8930 ARM processor (known as the Apple A4) and 256 MB of RAM. As with all the iPad device family, there are two distinct versions: the first one is equipped only with Wi-Fi 802.11 a/b/g/n connection, while the second one is also equipped with 3G UMTS/HSDPA/EDGE and a GPS. The two models are identified by model number A1219 (Wi-Fi only) and A1337 (Wi-Fi and 3G), while both models are characterized by the string iPad1,1. From a software point of view, it originally used the iPhone OS 3.2. The latest supported version is iOS 5.1.1.

iPad 2

The second model of iPad, known as **iPad 2**, is equipped with a 1 GHz S5L8940 ARM processor (known as Apple A5) and 512 MB of RAM. Compared to the previous version, Apple introduced a front and a rear camera of 0.75 MP. It was produced in three models: Wi-Fi only (model number A1395), Wi-Fi and GSM (model number A1396), and Wi-Fi and CDMA (model number A1397). There are four hardware strings: iPad2,1 (Wi-Fi only); iPad2,2 (Wi-Fi and GSM); iPad2,3 (CDMA and Wi-Fi); and iPad2,4 (Wi-Fi only with S5L8942 processor, known as A5 Rev A). With regards to the software, it originally used iOS 4.3. Currently, it is still supported by the latest version available (iOS 8.1).

iPad 3 (the new iPad)

The third model of iPad, known as **iPad 3** (or **the new iPad**), is equipped with a 1 GHz S5L8945 ARM processor (known as Apple A5X) and 1 GB of RAM memory. It was produced in three models: Wi-Fi only (model number A1416), Wi-Fi and cellular (VZ) (model number A1403), and cellular and Wi-Fi (model number A1430). There are three hardware strings of identification: iPad3,1 (Wi-Fi only); iPad3,2 (Wi-Fi, GSM, and CDMA); and iPad3,3 (Wi-Fi and GSM). With regards to the software, it originally used iOS 5.1. Currently, it is still supported by the latest version available (iOS 8.1).

iPad 4 (with Retina display)

The fourth model of iPad, known as iPad 4 (or iPad with Retina display), is equipped with a 1.4 GHz S5L8955 ARM processor (known as Apple A6X) and 1 GB of RAM. It was produced in three models: Wi-Fi only (model number A1458), Wi-Fi and cellular (MM) (model number A1460), and cellular and Wi-Fi (model number A1459). There are three hardware strings of identification: iPad3,4 (Wi-Fi only); iPad3,5 (Wi-Fi and GSM); and iPad 3,6 (Wi-Fi, GSM, and CDMA). With regards to the software, it originally used iOS 6.0.1. Currently, it is still supported by the latest version available (iOS 8.1).

iPad Air

The fifth model of iPad, known as **iPad Air**, is equipped with a 1.4 GHz S5L8965 ARM processor (known as Apple A7) and 1 GB of RAM memory. It was produced in two models: Wi-Fi only (model number A1474) and cellular and Wi-Fi (model number A1475). There are two hardware strings of identification: iPad4,1 (Wi-Fi only) and iPad4,2 (Wi-Fi and cellular). With regards to the software, it originally used iOS 7.0.3. Currently, it is still supported by the latest version available (iOS 8.1).

iPad mini

The first model of iPad mini, a smaller version of the iPad, is known simply as **iPad mini**. It is equipped with a 1 GHz S5L8942 ARM processor (known as the Apple A5 Rev A) and 512 MB of RAM. It was produced in three models: Wi-Fi only (model number A1432); Wi-Fi and GSM (model number A1454); and Wi-Fi, GSM and CDMA (model number A1455). There are three hardware strings of identification: iPad2,5 (Wi-Fi only); iPad2,6 (Wi-Fi and GSM); and iPad2,7 (Wi-Fi, GSM, and CDMA). With regards to the software, it originally used iOS 6.0.1. It is currently still supported by the latest version available at the time of writing the book (iOS 8.1).

iPad mini second generation

The second model of iPad mini, known as **iPad mini second generation** (or **iPad mini with Retina display**), is equipped with a 1.3 GHz S5L8960 ARM processor (known as Apple A7) and 1 GB of RAM. Compared to its predecessor, it uses a Retina screen and an Apple M7 motion coprocessor. It was produced in two models: Wi-Fi only (model number A1489), and Wi-Fi and cellular (model number A1490). There are three hardware strings of identification: iPad4,4 (Wi-Fi only); iPad4,5; and iPad4,6 (Wi-Fi and cellular). With regards to the software, it originally used iOS 7.0.3. It is currently still supported by the latest version available (iOS 8.1).

iPad mini third generation

The third model of iPad mini, known as **iPad mini third generation**, is equipped with a 1.3 GHz S5L8960 ARM processor (known as Apple A7) and 1 GB of RAM. Compared to its predecessor, it uses a Retina screen and an Apple M7 motion coprocessor. It was produced in three models: Wi-Fi only (model number A1599), Wi-Fi, and cellular (model number A1600 and A1601). There are three hardware strings of identification: iPad4,7 (Wi-Fi only); iPad4,8; and iPad4,9 (Wi-Fi and cellular). With regards to the software, it originally used iOS 8.0. It is currently still supported by the latest version available (iOS 8.1).

iPod touch

The iPod touch device is a media player that looks like the iPhone and uses the iOS operating system. It can play media and video games. It includes a Wi-Fi connection so that it can access the Internet with the mobile version of Safari, purchase songs online from the iTunes Store, and download apps from the App Store.

iPod touch (first model)

The first model of iPod touch, known simply as **iPod touch**, is equipped with a 620 MHz S5L8900 ARM processor and 128 MB of RAM memory. It is identified by the model number A1213 and by the hardware string iPod1,1. With regards to the software, it originally used iPhone OS 1.1. The latest supported version is iPhone OS 3.1.3.

iPod touch (second generation)

The second model of iPod touch, known as **iPod touch (second generation)**, is equipped with a 620 MHz S5L8720 ARM processor and 128 MB of RAM memory. It is identified by the model number A1288 and by the hardware string iPod2,1. With regards to the software, it originally used iPhone OS 2.1.1. The latest supported version is iOS 4.2.1.

iPod touch (third generation)

The third model of iPod touch, known as **iPod touch (third generation)**, is equipped with an 833 MHz S5L8920 ARM processor and 256 MB of RAM memory. It is identified by the model number A1318 and by the hardware string iPod3,1. With regards to the software, it originally used iPhone OS 3.1. The latest supported version is iOS 5.1.1.

iPod touch (fourth generation)

The fourth model of iPod touch, known as **iPod touch (fourth generation)**, is equipped with a 1 GHz S5L8930 ARM processor (known as Apple A4) and 256 MB of RAM memory. It is identified by the model number A1367 and by the hardware string iPod4,1. With regards to the software, it originally used iOS 4.1. The latest supported version is iOS 6.1.6.

iPod touch (fifth generation)

The fifth model of iPod touch, known as **iPod touch (fifth generation)**, is equipped with a 1 GHz S5L8942 ARM processor (known as Apple A5) and 512 MB of RAM memory. It is identified by the model number A1421 or A1509 and by the hardware string iPod5,1. With regards to the software, it originally used iOS 6.0. It is currently still supported by the latest version available (iOS 8.0).

iOS devices matrix

Some useful information about the iOS devices can be found at the following links:

- **iOS models** (http://theiphonewiki.com/wiki/Models): This page contains detailed tables with device name, device model, FCC-ID, internal name, and hardware identifier
- **Application Processor** (http://theiphonewiki.com/wiki/Application_Processor): This page contains a detailed processor list installed on the iOS devices

- **iPhone** (http://theiphonewiki.com/wiki/IPhone): This page contains a detailed table with all the features and characteristics for every iPhone model

- **iPad** (http://theiphonewiki.com/wiki/IPad): This page contains a detailed table with all the features and characteristics for every iPad model

- **iPod touch** (http://theiphonewiki.com/wiki/IPod_touch): This page contains a detailed table with all the features and characteristics for every iPod touch model

- **iOS Support Matrix** (http://iossupportmatrix.com/): This page contains a visual representation of all the iDevice models with their hardware and software features and support

- **iPhone IMEI** (http://iphoneimei.info/): This page contains a search engine to find the specific iPhone model from the IMEI number

- **IMEI.info** (http://www.imei.info/): This link is similar to the preceding link

- **iPhoneox** (http://www.iphoneox.com/): This link is similar to the preceding link

iOS operating system

All the devices described in this chapter have in common the use of the iOS operating system. Originally known as iPhone OS up to Version 3, it was developed by Apple specifically for iPhone, iPad, and iPod touch. It was unveiled for the first time in January 2007 and was introduced with the first model of iPhone in June of the same year.

iOS is an operating system, based on the older forefather Mac OS X, a derivative of BSD Unix with a Mach kernel XNU based on Darwin OS. It uses four levels of abstraction:

- **Core OS**: This level consists of file system, memory management, security, power management, TCP/IP, sockets, and encryption

- **Core services**: This level consists of networking, SQLite, geolocation, and threads

- **Media**: This level consists of OpenAL, audio, image, video, and OpenGL

- **Cocoa touch**: This level consists of core animation, multitasking, and gesture recognizer

The main screen, known as SpringBoard, is divided into three parts:

- The top bar that displays the telephone signal, any 3G/Wi-Fi/Bluetooth active connections, and the battery status
- The central part containing the icons of the applications in your device
- The bar at the bottom containing the most frequently-used applications

    ○ iPhone: Phone, Mail, Safari, Music
    ○ iPad/iPod touch: Messages, Mail, Safari, Music

The home screen appears whenever the user unlocks the device or presses the Home button while in another app.

The complete list of all the operating system versions produced by Apple is published and frequently updated at `http://theiphonewiki.com/wiki/Firmware`. At `http://www.ipswdownloader.com/`, it is possible to download all firmware for all models.

iDevice identification

It is very useful for a forensic investigator to be able to recognize the specific model of an iOS device while conducting a search and seizure or prior to an acquisition activity.

The recognition phase can be performed in four ways:

- Identifying the shape of the device and the connector used
- Checking the model number printed on the back of the device
- Connecting the device to a laptop and directly communicating with it
- Directly through the OS by tapping on **Settings | General | About**

The first method can be used by practicing the identification of the unique characteristics of each model. In some cases, it may be a complex assessment and it is therefore advisable to confirm the first evaluation with one of the other three methods.

The second method requires you to identify, on the back of the device, the model number. As reported in the previous tables from the model number, it is easy to identify the type of device. In the example shown in the following screenshot, it is possible to identify the model as an A1303 or an iPhone 3GS with 16 GB memory:

The third method is to retrieve the information directly, interacting with the device connected to a computer. As we will explore later on, once you turn on an iDevice, it can be password-protected and present a view to insert the lock code. Regardless of the knowledge of the code or the ability to overcome it or violate it, the device can communicate some information when connected to a computer.

Very useful in this context is the collection of tools and libraries available at http://www.libimobiledevice.org/ and preinstalled in the Linux distributions Santoku (https://santoku-linux.com/) and DEFT 8.1 (http://www.deftlinux.net).

Using the ideviceinfo command, it is possible to extract some information from the device, with no need to unlock it.

The information that can be extracted is as follows:

- Device name
- Device class
- Hardware model
- iOS version
- Telephony capability
- Unique device ID
- Wi-Fi MAC address

In the example shown in the following screenshot, it is possible to identify that the connected device is a Wi-Fi only iPad mini 1 (hardware model P105AP) with OS 6.1.2 (build 10B146) called "iPad di Mattia":

iOS file system

All the iDevices use HFSX as their file system, a variant case of HFS+. Within the same folder, then, it is possible to store two or more files with the same name, but different from the case of each individual character (for example, iOS.jpg and ios.jpg).

The HFS+ file system

HFS Plus (or HFS+) is the file system developed by Apple to replace, from Mac OS 8.1, HFS as the default file system for Mac computers. In Apple's official documentation, it is called Mac OS Extended.

HFS+ is an improved version of HFS, which allows the user to support larger files (thanks to block addresses of 32 bits instead of 16 bits) and uses Unicode for the names of file system objects (files and folders), thus allowing up to 255 characters for each. Until Mac OS X Tiger, HFS+ only supported Unix file system privileges to access the file. The Tiger version introduced support for security checks based on **Access Control List (ACL)**, typical of Microsoft environments.

The HFS+ volumes are allocation blocks that may contain one or more sectors (typically 512 bytes in a hard drive). The number of allocation blocks depends on the total size of the volume. The HFS+ file system uses 32 bits to address the allocation blocks, thus allowing access to 232 blocks (4,294,967,296).

A typical HFS+ volume is defined by the following six major data structures that contain the information needed to manage the data volume:

- `Volume Header File`: This file defines the basic structure of the volume, as the size of each allocation block, the number of used and free blocks, and the size and position of the other special files

- `Allocation File`: This file includes a bitmap with the used and unused blocks within a volume

- `Catalog File`: This file defines the structure of the directories in the file system and it is used to identify the location of a specific file or folder

- `Extents Overflow File`: This file contains pointers to additional extents for files that require more than eight contiguous allocation blocks

- `Attributes File`: This file contains the customizable attributes of a file

- `Startup File`: This file contains the information required at system boot

The data structure can be represented as follows:

Reserved (1024 bytes)
Volume Header
Allocation File
Extents Overflow File
Catalog File
Attributes File
Startup File
Alternate Volume Header
Reserved (512 bytes)

Both the special and user file are stored in **forks** or in a set of allocation blocks. The space is usually allocated in **clumps**, where the size of a clump is a multiple of the size of a block. The contiguous allocation blocks for a given file are grouped into **extents**. Each extent is characterized by a starting allocation block and by the number of blocks, which indicates how many blocks contain data from that specific file.

In the `boot` blocks and `startup` files, the first 1024 bytes of a volume are reserved as boot blocks and may contain information requested during the startup of the system. Alternatively, boot information can be found within the `startup` file, which allows you to store a greater amount of information.

A `volume header` file, a 512 byte data structure, contains the volume information, including the location of other data structures. It is always located at the beginning of the block 2 or 1024 bytes after the beginning of the volume. A copy of the `volume header` file, called the **alternate volume header**, is 1024 bytes before the end of the volume. The first 1024 bytes and the last 512 bytes of the volume are reserved.

The information contained in a `volume header` file is as follows:

Field name	Size	Description
`signature`	2 bytes	This field implies the volume signature, which must be `'H+'`, if the volume is HSF Plus, and `'HX'`, if the volume is HFSX.
`version`	2 bytes	This field implies the format version, which is `'4'` for HFS Plus and `'5'` for HFSX.
`attributes`	4 bytes	This field implies the volume attributes (for example, journaling active).
`lastMountedVersion`	4 bytes	This field describes the operating system installed.
`journalInfoBlock`	4 bytes	This field is the allocation block that manages the journaling.
`createDate`	4 bytes	This field implies the volume creation date.
`modifyDate`	4 bytes	This field implies the volume last modified date.
`backupDate`	4 bytes	This field implies the volume last backup.
`checkedDate`	4 bytes	This field implies the volume last consistency check date.
`fileCount`	4 bytes	This field implies the number of file in the volume, without the special files.
`folderCount`	4 bytes	This field implies the number of folders in the volume, without the root folder.
`blockSize`	4 bytes	This field implies the allocation block size (bytes).
`totalBlocks`	4 bytes	This field implies the total number of allocation blocks.
`freeBlocks`	4 bytes	This field implies the number of available allocation blocks.
`nextAllocation`	4 bytes	This field implies the address of the next available allocation block.
`rsrcClumpSize`	4 bytes	This field implies the default clump size for a resource fork.
`dataClumpSize`	4 bytes	This field implies the default clump size for a data fork.

Field name	Size	Description
nextCatalogID	4 bytes	This field implies the first available CatalogID.
writeCount	4 bytes	This field implies the number of times the volume has been mounted.
encondingsBitmap	8 bytes	This bitmap describes the encoding used for file and folder name.
finderInfo	32 bytes	This field implies the information used by the Mac OS Finder and the system software boot process.
allocationFile	80 bytes	This field implies the location and the size of File Allocation.
extentsFile	80 bytes	This field implies the location and the size of the extents file.
catalogFile	80 bytes	This field implies the location and the size of the catalog file.
attributesFile	80 bytes	This field implies the location and the size of the attributes file.
startupFile	80 bytes	This field implies the location and the size of the startup file.

The allocation (bitmap) file is used to keep track of which allocation blocks on a volume are currently allocated to a structure (file or folder). It is a bitmap that contains one bit for each allocation block in the volume. If a bit is 1, the corresponding allocation block is in use. If the bit is 0, the corresponding allocation block is not currently in use and is therefore available to be assigned to a file or folder.

The catalog file is used to keep the information on the hierarchy of files and folders on HFS+. A catalog file is organized as a binary tree (type B-Tree) and therefore consists of head node, index nodes, and leaf nodes. The position of the first block of the catalog file (and thus the head node of the file) is stored in the volume header file. The catalog file contains the metadata of all the files and folders on a volume, including creation, modification and access date, permissions, file identifier, and information about the user that created the file.

The data structure for each file in the `catalog` file is as follows:

```
struct HFSPlusCatalogFile {
    SInt16              recordType;
    UInt16              flags;
    UInt32              reserved1;
    HFSCatalogNodeID    fileID;
    UInt32              createDate;
    UInt32              contentModDate;
    UInt32              attributeModDate;
    UInt32              accessDate;
    UInt32              backupDate;
    HFSPlusBSDInfo      permissions;
    FileInfo            userInfo;
    ExtendedFileInfo    finderInfo;
    UInt32              textEncoding;
    UInt32              reserved2;
    HFSPlusForkData     dataFork;
    HFSPlusForkData     resourceFork;
};
```

The two areas of most interest to identify the location of the files are `dataFork` and `resourceFork` (both of the type `HFSPlusForkData`).

The `dataFork` field contains information about the location and size of a file or the current contents of the file, while the `resourceFork` field contains the application metadata of the file.

The `HFSPlusForkData` data structure is defined by four fields as follows:

```
struct HFSPlusForkData {
    UInt64               logicalSize;
    UInt32               clumpSize;
    UInt32               totalBlocks;
    HFSPlusExtentRecord  extents;
};
```

The `logicalSize` field defines the size in bytes of the data, the `totalBlocks` field defines the number of blocks allocated, the `extents` field stores the first eight extents of a file descriptor (an extent is a contiguous segment of a file). If a file requires a greater number of descriptor extents, these are stored in the `extents overflow` file. Each extent that composes a file is described in the `HFSPlusExtentDescriptor` data structure and is defined by the two fields as follows:

```
struct HFSPlusExtentDescriptor {
    UInt32              startBlock;
    UInt32              blockCount;
};
```

The `startBlock` field identifies the first allocation block in an extent while the `blockCount` field identifies the length in number of allocation blocks of an extent. The start offset of a file can then be determined by finding the first extent and multiplying the corresponding `startBlock` field to the size of the allocation block, which is defined in the `volume header` file. Since the files cannot always be completely stored in contiguous blocks on the disk and may be fragmented, `HFS+` `dataFork` defines a structure that holds up to eight extents. When a file requires more than eight extents, it uses the `extents overflow` file, which combines the file with additional extents.

For the `extents overflow` file, if a file in an HFS+ volume is composed by more than eight extents (or is fragmented over more than eight contiguous positions of the volume), the extents in excess will be stored in the `extents overflow` file. The file structure is similar to the `content` file (binary tree, B-Tree); however, it's greatly simplified by the presence of a single data structure (`HFSPlusExtentKey`).

The `attributes` file enables the direct management through the file system of additional attributes for a file. The attributes are defined as key/value pairs.

An interesting concept associated with HFS+ is the file system journaling used for a recovery process after a volume was not safely unmounted. This file stores file transactions (`create`, `delete`, `modify`, and so on) and might contain the same metadata stored in the `attributes` or in the `catalog` file. It is activated by default on the iOS devices and can be used to recover deleted content.

Device partitions

iDevices use a NAND type memory divided into two partitions: the system or firmware partition, and the data partition.

The system partition contains the iOS operating system and all the preinstalled applications and it is identified as /dev/disk0s1 or /dev/disk0s1s1. This partition is not generally accessible to the user in the write mode and may only be modified by an update of the operating system. Since it cannot contain user-installed applications and data, it is small (1-2 GB depending on the specific model).

The data partition occupies most of the space in the NAND memory and is identified as /dev/disk0s2 or /dev/disk0s2s2. The partition contains user data and user-installed applications and is mounted at run time by the operating system inside /private/var.

System partition

If the device is in a normal condition, all information relevant to an investigation is within the partition containing user data. The system partition is therefore not usually of interest. A complete description of the folder content is available at http://theiphonewiki.com/wiki/ and the partition will look like the following screenshot:

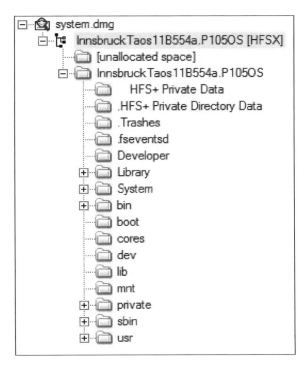

It should be noted, however, that /private/etc/passwd (shown in the following screenshot) contains the password of the users configured on the device (mobile and root):

For all iDevices, the default password for the mobile and root users is **alpine**. This password cannot be modified by the user, unless they are performing the jailbreaking operations, as shown in the following screenshot:

```
##
# User Database
#
# This file is the authoritative user database.
##
nobody:*:-2:-2:Unprivileged User:/var/empty:/usr/bin/false
root:/smx7MYTQIi2M:0:0:System Administrator:/var/root:/bin/sh
mobile:/smx7MYTQIi2M:501:501:Mobile User:/var/mobile:/bin/sh
```

Data partition

The structure of the data partition has changed over the different evolutions of the operating system. The following screenshot shows an example of the folder structure extracted from a jailbroken iPad mini 1G running iOS 7.0.4:

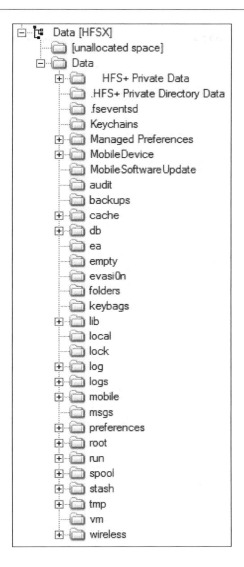

The useful elements for the analysis of an iDevice will be discussed in *Chapter 4, Analyzing iOS Devices*. It is considered useful to point out that the iDevice devices use the Property List and SQLite databases as data and configuration containers.

The property list file

The property list files (also known as plist) are used by Apple for the management of the configuration of the operating system and key applications. Typically, these are simple text files formatted in XML. In most cases, a plist file contains the text strings and Boolean values; in some cases, it can contain data encoded in the binary format, as shown in the following screenshot. Although they can be easily analyzed using a simple text editor, it is more convenient to browse the hierarchical structure through a dedicated reader.

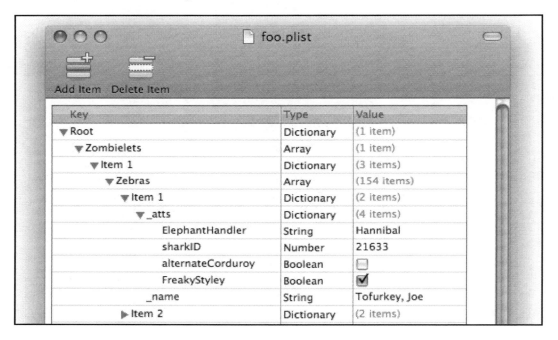

In the Mac environment, it is possible to install the freeware tool **Property List Editor** developed by Apple. It can be downloaded from the website of the XCode development platform (https://developer.apple.com/xcode/).

In a Windows environment, we can use **plist Editor for Windows** (http://www.icopybot.com/plist-editor.htm).

SQLite database

The iOS devices use SQLite databases to store information and user data. The analysis of these files requires a minimum knowledge of the SQL commands for the selection of data; however, there are several free software options that can interpret and easily display the data in a database. An example of cross-platform software is **SQLite Database Browser** (`http://sqlitebrowser.org/`), which allows us to visualize the structure of the database and to navigate within the data, as shown in the following screenshot:

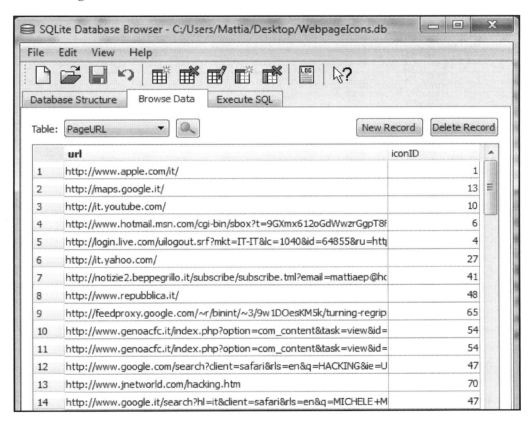

In a Windows environment, it is also advisable to use the software **SQLite Expert** (available in both personal and commercial licenses at `http://www.sqliteexpert.com/`).

Summary

This chapter illustrated the features of interest for iOS devices during mobile forensic activities. In particular, it introduced the different models with guidance on recognition techniques based on the model number or hardware model number. It also contained an introduction to the iOS operating system with particular reference to the file system (HFSX), the partitions (system and data), and the main data structures (property list files and SQLite database). These topics are the basics for forensic activity on an iDevice and will be used in the next chapters when dealing with acquisition and analysis.

Self-test questions

1. What is the latest supported version of iOS for iPhone 4?

    1. iOS 5.1.1
    2. iOS 6.1.2
    3. iOS 7.1.2
    4. iOS 8.1.2

2. Which are the model numbers associated with iPhone 6?

    1. A1522 and A1524
    2. A1549 and A1586
    3. A1528 and A1530
    4. A1428 and A1429

3. What file system does iOS use?

    1. NTFS
    2. EXT3
    3. HFS+
    4. HFSX

4. What metafile is used to keep information on files and folders in iOS file system?

    1. Volume Header
    2. Allocation
    3. Catalog
    4. Extent

5. What is the default root user password?

    1. apple
    2. iphone
    3. leopard
    4. alpine

6. What kind of file is mostly used to keep iOS configuration?

    1. Text
    2. Json
    3. Plist
    4. HTML

3
Evidence Acquisition from iDevices

The purpose of this chapter is to introduce techniques and tools used for the acquisition of data from an iDevice. In the first part of the chapter, the boot process, the data security features, and the encryption used by Apple are shown. The second part deals with the different acquisition methods (direct, backup/logical, advanced logical, and physical), providing a description of state-of-the-art techniques for the cracking of the lock code or the overcoming of it. Finally, in the last part, we introduce the concept of jailbreaking, which is useful for physical acquisition of the latest devices.

iOS boot process and operating modes

The boot process for an iOS device is composed of three steps: **Low Level Bootloader (LLB)**, **iBoot**, and **iOS kernel**. To guarantee the integrity of the different components, all the steps involved in the boot process are signed. The signature for LLB is verified by the Apple Root CS public key, contained in the Boot ROM code. Then, LLB verifies and executes iBoot, which then verifies and executes the iOS kernel. In this way, it is ensured that all the components are signed by Apple. There are a lot of studies, papers, and books related to the iOS boot process and how to overcome the protections implemented by Apple (you can find all the details in *Appendix A, References*). We suggest reading the latest version of the Apple paper, *iOS Security, Apple, October 2014*.

From the point of view of a forensic analyst, it is important to know that iDevices can operate in the following three different ways:

- **Normal**: This mode is the traditional iOS user interface.

- **Recovery**: This mode is used to perform activation and upgrades on an iDevice. It can be activated by holding down the Home button on a powered off device and connecting it to a computer via the USB cable.

- **Device Firmware Upgrade (DFU)**: This mode is used by an iDevice during the iOS upgrades and when one of the processes in verification boot chain fails. It can be activated by holding down the Home and the Power button together (with the device powered on or off) for 10 seconds, and then it is necessary to release the Power button and hold the Home button for 10 seconds more.

Both **Recovery** and **DFU** modes are really useful for the physical acquisition of iDevices, as we will show in the dedicated section.

iOS data security

A complete description of iOS data security is out of the scope of this book, but we wish to give you just an overview (taken from the Apple paper *iOS Security* and from Christian D'Orazio's thesis, see *Appendix A, References*) of hardware and software security features.

Hardware security features

Every iDevice, starting from iPhone 3GS, has a dedicated AES 256-bit crypto engine built in between the flash storage and the main system memory. The purposes of this processor are to accelerate the encryption and decryption operations and to protect user data so that they remain encrypted on the device's flash memory. A **unique ID (UID)** is associated with each device and allows data to be cryptographically tied to a particular device. The UID cannot be read directly and it is used as AES 256-bit key to generate encryption keys that protect user data. These encryption keys, known as **EMF** and **Dkey (Class D Key)** are stored in a specific area of the flash memory, called **PLOG block** (or **Effaceable Storage**). When the device deletes this area it makes the whole volume unreadable and the content is completely and definitely encrypted with no way to recover it.

File data protection

As described by Apple in their paper, *iOS Security* (see *Appendix A, References*):

> "*In addition to the hardware encryption features built into iOS devices, Apple uses a technology called Data Protection to further protect data stored in flash memory on the device.*"

Apple implements an encrypted HFS+ volume, in which each file is assigned to a class, depending on the type of data and security level required. The paper states that:

> "*Every time a file on the data partition is created, Data Protection creates a new 256-bit key (the "per-file" key) and gives it to the hardware AES engine, which uses the key to encrypt the file as it is written to flash memory using AES CBC mode.*"

The per-file key is then wrapped with the key of the class to which the file belongs. The wrapped per-file key is stored in the `cprotect` attribute, which is part of the file's metadata contained in the `Attributes` file. The paper states that:

> "*When a file is opened, its metadata is decrypted with the file system key, revealing the wrapped per-file key and a notation on which class protects it. The per-file key is unwrapped with the class key, then supplied to the hardware AES engine, which decrypts the file as it is read from flash memory.*"

It is important to note that the file system key can be erased and in that case the content of every file becomes definitely unreadable. There are four basic classes that use different policies to determine when file content is accessible and where the class keys are stored. With the exception of the Dkey, all class keys are stored in the system **Keybag**, which is a file that contains master keys for each one of the classes available, as shown in the following screenshot:

Class ID	Name	Key Availability	Class Key Stored in	Class Key protected with
A	NSFileProtectionComplete	When device unlocked	Keybag	passcode + UID
B	NSFileProtectionCompleteUnlessOpen	While device locked	Keybag	passcode + UID
C	NSFileProtectionCompleteUntilFirstUserAuthentication	After first unlock	Keybag	passcode + UID
D	NSFileProtectionNone	Always	PLOG	UID-derived key (Key0x835)

Class D offers the lowest security level because the Dkey is not derived from the passcode but wrapped in the **PLOG** area with a value (**Key0x835**) that can be retrieved by communicating with the kernel. From a forensics point of view, it is important to note that all the files created by a native iOS application, except e-mail messages and related attachments, belong to Class D. It means that all the cryptographic keys required to decrypt a file can be retrieved without knowing or cracking the passcode.

Unique device identifier

Every single iDevice produced is identified by a **Unique Device ID (UDID)**. As well explained in The iPhone Wiki (`http://theiphonewiki.com/wiki/UDID`), it can be calculated as the **SHA-1** hash of a particular 60- or 59-character long string that can be obtained as follows:

- An 11-character or 12-character long (on newer devices) serial number (exactly like it is written in the **Settings** app).
- A 15-character long IMEI number without spaces (on older devices), empty string for iPod touch, and the Wi-Fi model iPad devices, or a 13-character ECID in decimal with no leading zeroes (on newer devices).

  The **ECID** is the **Electronic Chip ID**. For more information, refer to `https://theiphonewiki.com/wiki/ECID`.

- A 17-character long Wi-Fi MAC address (letters in lowercase, including colons). For the iPod touch first generation, use `00:00:00:00:00:00`.
- A 17-character long Bluetooth MAC address (letters in lowercase, including colons).

Case study – UDID calculation on iPhone 4s

On iPhone 4s, the UDID is calculated as follows:

SHA1 (serial number + ECID converted to decimal + Wi-Fi MAC address + Bluetooth MAC address)

If the device is unlocked, the serial number, Wi-Fi MAC address, and Bluetooth can be obtained by tapping **Settings | General | About** on the device's main screen, as shown in the following screenshot:

Serial Number	DNRJ9Z9SDTC0
Wi-Fi Address	84:FC:FE:D3:AC:E2
Bluetooth	84:FC:FE:D3:AC:8D

The ECID can be obtained as follows:

1. Put the device in **Recovery** mode.
2. Open Windows **Device Manager**, go to **Universal Serial Bus controllers | Apple Mobile Device USB Driver**, right-click on it and select **Properties**.
3. Click on **Details**, search and select **Device Instance Path** in the drop-down menu, and copy the text to a text file.
4. On a Mac OS X, navigate to **System Information | System Report** and look in the USB entry under **Hardware**.

In this example we have the following entries:

- **Serial number**: DNRJ9Z9SDTC0
- **ECID**: 00000032CD418838B
- **Wi-Fi MAC address**: 84:FC:CE:D3:AC:E2
- **Bluetooth MAC address**: 84:FC:CE:D3:AC:8D

Before calculating the UDID, we need to convert the hex value for ECID to a decimal number, so 32CD418838B corresponds to 3491071820683.

The UDID can be calculated as follows:

```
SHA1(DNRJ9Z9SDTC0349107182068384:fc:fe:d3:ac:e284:fc:fe:d3:ac:8d) =
26ccdbcb74b2ab8e9e97aa096883a10442c6f2ef
```

The calculated value can be verified using iTunes, after connecting the device to the computer, as shown in the following screenshot:

Otherwise, the UDID can also be verified using the `ideviceinfo` tool introduced in *Chapter 2, Introduction to iOS Devices*, as shown in the following screenshot:

```
deft8 ~ % ideviceinfo -s
BasebandCertId: 2
BasebandKeyHashInformation:
 AKeyStatus: 2
 SKeyHash: 7MQEUyvzG4gjjZc7KsNNAVTS8g4=
 SKeyStatus: 0
BasebandSerialNumber: JxnwkQ==
BasebandVersion: 5.2.00
BoardId: 8
BuildVersion: 11D201
ChipID: 35136
DeviceClass: iPhone
DeviceColor: black
DeviceName: EpiPhone
DevicePublicKey: LS0tLS1CRUdJTiBSU0EgUFVCTElDIEtFWS0tLS0tCk1JR0pBb0dCQUtHUjZMOUM
weE56dlhaNmdQd3hleUF1RUJGUjlQYm1mUmlNdTIvaDliOWppZXJpVVFYWnVFTE4KampZeW0zVVQvbnd
Za0hNOFhsVWx2YUJtMWdJS2NveW1yOE5JbVvd3S2N5ak41b2pEbDE5NnJhWlBqUmZEVVJXYQpsUXVUC8
4SDZTRFJ2N0NianU2OEg0MFJocURJY1Njbi9oUXAvd2s5Q2IydHdxWlFppQnNKQWdNQkFBRT0KLS0tLS1
FTkQgUlNBIFBVQkxJQyBLRVktLS0tLQo=
DieID: 2242306697049237152
HardwareModel: N94AP
PartitionType:
ProductVersion: 7.1.1
ProductionSOC: true
ProtocolVersion: 2
TelephonyCapability: true
UniqueChipID: 3491071820683
UniqueDeviceID: 26ccdbcb74b2ab8e9e97aa096883a10442c6f2ef
UntrustedHostBUID: 0BD553BE-17EB-544C-0626-47E8AE883479
WiFiAddress: 84:fc:fe:d3:ac:e2
```

Lockdown certificate

The first time you connect an unlocked iDevice to a computer and run the iTunes software, a pairing/sync certificate, known as a **lockdown** certificate, is created on the computer's hard drive. Depending on the operating system in which iTunes is installed, lockdown certificates are stored in the following folders:

- **Windows 7/8**: C:\Program Data\Apple\Lockdown
- **Windows Vista**: C:\Users\[username]\AppData\roaming\Apple Computer\Lockdown
- **Windows XP**: C:\Documents and Settings\[username]\Application Data\Apple Computer\Lockdown
- **Mac OS X**: /var/db/lockdown

Within these paths, there is a lockdown certificate for each device that was ever connected to the computer. The certificate is a plist file called <UDID>.plist, where UDID corresponds with the unique identifier of the iDevice, as shown in the following screenshot:

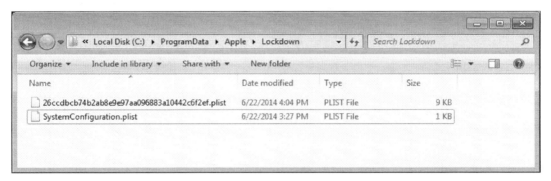

Once the certificate has been generated, you will no longer need to unlock the iDevice when you connect it to the computer and some of its content will be made available. The lockdown certificate remains valid until the user resets their device to factory settings. Of fundamental importance to the forensic acquisition of data is the fact that the certificate can be copied to another machine, and then you have partial access to the device even without knowing the lock code.

Starting from iOS 7.0, when you connect a device, two pop-up authorizations are displayed. The first popup appears on the computer in iTunes and it asks the user to click on **Continue**:

The second popup appears on the iDevice screen once unlocked, and requires the user to click on the **Trust** button to allow pairing with the computer.

Search and seizure

If you have to deal with a search and seizure of an iDevice, it is really important to perform at least three steps, as follows:

1. Turn on **Airplane Mode** from **Settings**.

2. If the device is unlocked, set **Auto-Lock** to **Never** from **Settings | General | Auto-Lock**.

3. Check whether the passcode is set or not from **Settings | Passcode**.

    1. If the passcode is set, acquire the content from the device as soon as possible (at least a logical acquisition) or keep the device charged.

    2. If the passcode is not set, turn it off.

4. If the device is locked or you identified that a passcode is set, seize any computer that was used to synchronize, or simply authorize the iDevice because there you can possibly find a lockdown certificate that will allow access to the data even if the device is protected with a passcode.

iOS device acquisition

Once you identified the specific model that you need to acquire, it becomes important to understand the best technique to use. The type of acquisition depends basically on the following five parameters:

* Model
* iOS version
* Passcode (not set, simple passcode, or complex passcode)
* Presence of a backup password
* Is the device jailbroken?

Nowadays, in the forensic community the following four techniques are used to access data stored on iDevices:

* **Direct**: This technique consists of a direct interaction with a powered on device through non-forensic software
* **Backup or logical acquisition**: This technique consists of a partial file system acquisition through the iTunes backup or using a forensic acquisition tool that uses the iTunes libraries
* **Advanced logical**: This technique is based on lockdown services and was introduced for the first time by the researcher Jonathan Zdziarski
* **Physical**: This technique generates a traditional forensic image for both the system and data partition

Direct acquisition

The direct acquisition can be carried out with all iDevices, regardless of the operating system version. It requires that the device is not protected with a passcode, the passcode is known, or the analyst has a lockdown certificate. To make a direct acquisition, you can use various types of software known as iDevice browsers. Keep in mind that *this activity is performed with a non-forensic tool that also permits writing operations, so the analyst must operate very carefully to avoid accidental erasure.* The most used tools on Windows and Mac for this type of acquisition are **iFunBox, iMazing, iExplorer,** and **WonderShare Dr.Fone**. These tools require the installation of an updated version of iTunes because they use its libraries to communicate with the device. Before connecting the device to your computer, you should ensure that in **iTunes | Preferences | Devices**, the **Prevent iPods, iPhones, and iPads from syncing automatically** option is enabled, as shown in the following screenshot:

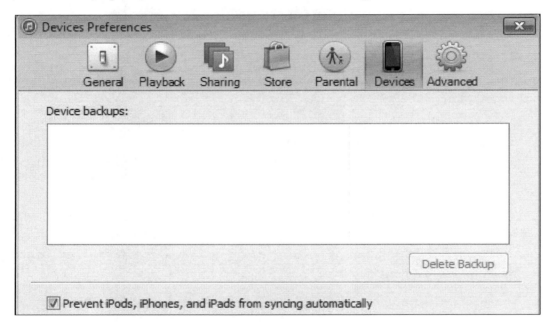

Backup or logical acquisition

Backup or logical acquisition allows the analyst to recover more information than direct acquisition and in a more forensics way as it creates a backup for the device without altering any data. Regarding the passcode, the conditions are similar to what is explained for direct acquisition: the analyst must know the passcode or have a lockdown certificate to perform this kind of acquisition. Before connecting the device, you also need to disable automatic syncing in the iTunes software. This acquisition can be performed in two ways: using iTunes or using forensic software.

Acquisition with iTunes backup

The acquisition through iTunes can be done in a very simple way using the backup function of the device. Once you start iTunes, you need to click on the name of the device to access detailed information. At this point, you need to check how the device is configured in relation to the backup operation. There may be the following three cases:

- The device is configured to perform a local backup not protected by a password
- The device is configured to perform a local backup with a password previously set by the device owner
- The device is configured to backup to iCloud

In the first two cases, simply click on the **Back Up Now** button to start the backup on the computer, as shown in the following screenshot:

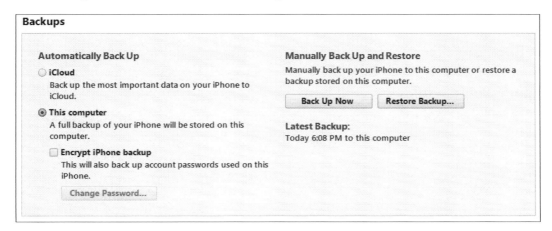

If the user has not chosen a password, the created backup can be analyzed with various tools. Otherwise, the analyst needs to crack the backup password before starting the analysis. Both the password cracking and backup structures will be discussed in *Chapter 5, Evidence Acquisition and Analysis from iTunes Backup*.

In the third case, before starting the backup, the analyst must change the option from **iCloud** to **This Computer**. In this way, the backup will be performed locally and will not overwrite any existing data present in the previous backups on iCloud. The data acquisition from iCloud is explained in *Chapter 6, Evidence Acquisition and Analysis from iCloud*.

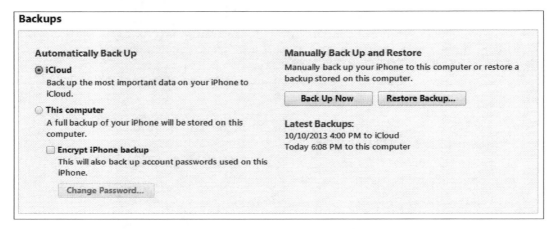

Logical acquisition with forensic tools

In the market, there are various forensic tools that can perform backup or logical acquisition, for example Cellebrite UFED 4PC/UFED Touch/UFED Physical Analyzer, Oxygen Forensic® Suite Standard/Analyst, Mobile Phone Examiner, MobilEdit!, Lantern, and XRY. For a detailed reference list, refer to *Appendix B, Tools for iOS Forensics*.

Case study – logical acquisition with Oxygen Forensic® Suite

The Oxygen Forensic® Suite software is a commercial product that allows the logical acquisition of an iOS device. It is available in two licensing modes: **Standard** and **Analyst**. On the Oxygen website, you can request a freeware version of the Standard license, which allows data to be extracted from the device but offers limited analysis capabilities. To start the extraction, it is necessary to click on the **Connect device** button from the main screen, as shown in the following screenshot:

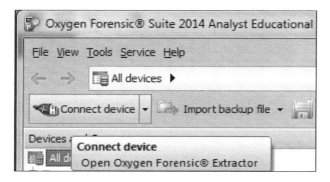

The software will then begin the extraction procedure, and you can choose the type of connection you want to start. You can choose between **Auto device connection** and **Manual device selection**, as shown in the following screenshot. For iDevices, it is generally sufficient to select the first option.

The software starts searching for a connected iDevice. If the device is locked with a passcode, the software asks the analyst to insert the passcode or to provide a lockdown certificate. The software provides the UDID for the iDevice, so it is easier for the analyst to search it on a computer previously synced with the device itself. If the analyst knows the passcode, he/she needs to insert it into the device, authorize the computer, and click on **I entered the passcode. Press to connect**. Otherwise, he/she can choose the **Select lockdown plist** option and provide the tool with the lockdown certificate.

If the certificate is correct, the software displays a confirmation screen with a button to start the connection to the device, as shown in the following screenshot:

At this point, the software displays information specific to the connected device (model, IMEI number, iOS version, and boot loader), as shown in the following screenshot:

The investigator can then enter information about the case, and if known, the backup password for the device.

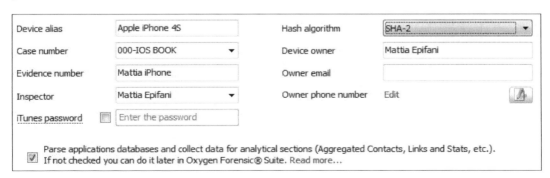

Then, the analyst can select the data they want to extract, by choosing the ones supported by this method, as shown in the following screenshot:

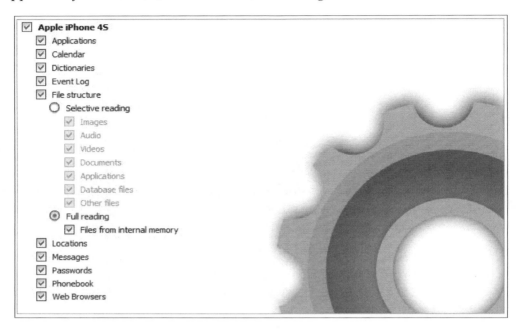

When clicking on the **Next** button, the acquisition procedure starts and displays a progress bar. It should be noted that during the extraction, the software also proceeds with parsing all the data found, including the search for deleted records within the database stored in the phone (for example, calls, SMS, chat, and so on). For this reason, the acquisition may require a large amount of time, but after that the analyst is ready to parse the data within the software, as shown in the following screenshot:

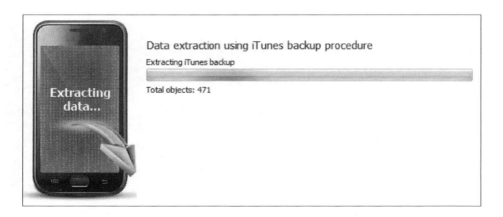

If the device has a backup password previously set by the user, Oxygen can work with **Passware Kit Forensic** (if installed on the computer used to acquire data) trying to make an attack on the backup password. If the examiner knows the password, he/she has the chance to finish the attack and enter it manually. At the end of the cracking process, if the password has been detected, the software proceeds with the extraction of all the data, in a similar way as described previously. If the password is not found, the software extracts only the multimedia content (images, video, books, and so on) and does not provide information about the applications preinstalled or installed by the user.

Advanced logical acquisition

The advanced logical acquisition method was first introduced by the iOS Security researcher Jonathan Zdziarski, in his tool, **Waterboard**, released in June 2013. The author's description in his article states that,

> *"Waterboard is an open source iOS forensic imaging tool, capable of performing an advanced logical acquisition of iOS devices by utilizing extended services and back doors in Apple's built-in lockdown services. These services can bypass Apple's mobile backup encryption and other encryption to deliver a clear text copy of much of the file system to any machine that can or has previously paired with the device."*

A detailed explanation can be found in the paper, *Identifying Back Doors, Attack Points, and Surveillance Mechanisms in iOS Devices, Jonathan Zdziarski* (see *Appendix A, References*). Currently, the Waterboard tool is no longer available and supported by Zdziarski, but there are few forensic tools offering the same feature: UFED Physical Analyzer, Oxygen Forensics Toolkit, and AccessData MPE.

Case study – advanced logical acquisition with UFED Physical Analyzer

UFED Physical Analyzer is a software product from Cellebrite UFED and supplied with the purchase of UFED Touch or UFED 4PC. The advanced logical acquisition in UFED Physical Analyzer can be started through the main interface of the software under the menu item, **Extract | iOS Device Extraction**, as shown in the following screenshot:

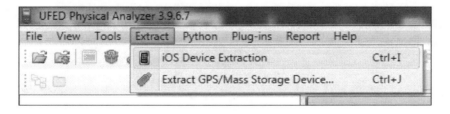

The analyst can now choose **Advanced Logical extraction**:

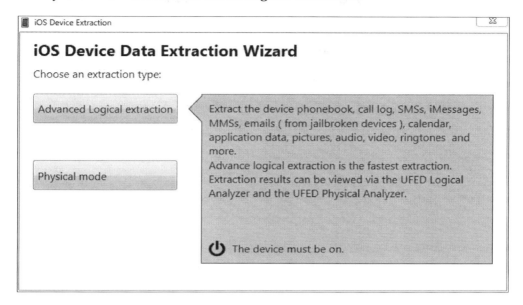

The software requires you to connect the turned-on device using the correct cable (30-pin connector or Lightning 8-pin connector), as follows:

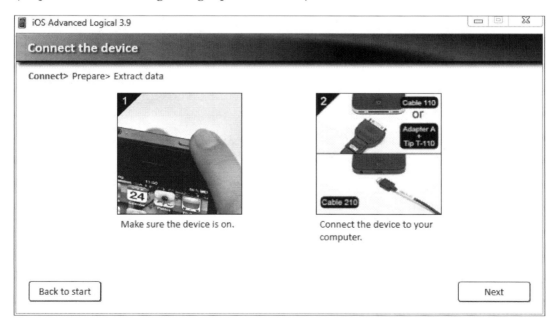

The device must be powered on and unlocked; otherwise, the software displays an error message stating **The iOS device is locked**. To proceed, the analyst must unlock the device with the passcode or copy the device lockdown certificate inside the correct folder.

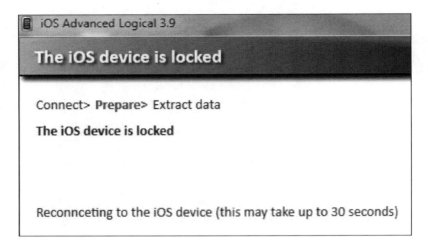

The software checks whether a password is set on the backup device and shows two possible methods for the acquisition: **Method 1** corresponds to a device backup or logical acquisition, while **Method 2** allows the analyst to extract data using the lockdown service (advanced logical acquisition).

If the device has a backup password with **Method 1**, the analyst must know the password or crack it (as explained in *Chapter 5*, *Evidence Acquisition and Analysis from iTunes Backup*), while with **Method 2**, it is possible to extract part of the data also without cracking the backup password. For this reason, when you need to acquire a device with a backup password, it is advisable to perform both acquisitions. In this way, you can definitely see some information thanks to **Method 2** and try to recover more details by cracking the encrypted acquisition carried out with **Method 1**.

Connect> **Prepare>** Extract data

The iTunes backup of this device (iPhone with iOS 7.1.1) is not encrypted.
The data extracted by each method will vary based on the device model and iOS version.

Method 1 — Extraction of a rich set of data including call logs, SMSs, MMSs, applications data, data files and notes. Recommended

Method 2 — Extraction of a rich set of data including SMSs, MMSs, applications data and data files. Some data types are not extracted (More info...). Extended extraction time.

Once you select the extraction method, the software initiates the procedure requiring the user to set the destination folder. Scanning takes a variable time depending on the chosen method (**Method 1** is performed in a single step and is faster than **Method 2**, which requires three steps), the memory size of the device, and the space occupied by files (especially media files such as pictures, videos, music, and so on).

Once the acquisition is complete, the software displays a report showing the amount of extracted data and the time taken, as shown in the following screenshot. From this window, the analyst can choose whether to return to the home screen or open the acquisition made in UFED Physical Analyzer for the analysis activities.

Connect> Prepare> **Extract data**

Extraction completed. ✓

Extraction size: 244,72 MB

Time elapsed: 00:57

Physical acquisition with forensic tools

Physical acquisition allows most of the content from an iOS device to be extracted. Unlike the backup or logical and advanced logical methods, the analyst can obtain a forensic copy of the device memory and access all the files stored there. Some examples of information of interest that can be retrieved only through a physical acquisition are the e-mail messages and log files of the device. The physical acquisition is based on hardware vulnerabilities during the boot process. For this reason, this operation is not invasive on the data stored on the iDevice because it directly uploads into RAM an alternative operating system through which it can launch acquisition commands. Currently, it is supported on the first iPhone model/3G/3GS/4, iPad 1, and iPod touch 1/2/3/4.

If the device is not protected by a passcode, the physical acquisition can be carried out without problems by creating an image of both system and data partitions.

If the iDevice is protected with a passcode, it is necessary to distinguish the following two cases:

- If the passcode is simple (4 digits), it can be cracked in 20 to 30 minutes, depending on the device type

- If the passcode is complex (multidigit or alphanumeric) the analyst has the following two options:

    ° Try a brute force or a dictionary attack on the passcode.

    ° Perform the physical acquisition without cracking the passcode. In this case, the physical acquisition will decode all the data whose encryption does not depend on the passcode, while other data (for example, e-mail, stored password, and so on) cannot be decrypted.

Several forensic tools can perform physical acquisition, such as iPhone data protection tools, UFED Physical Analyzer, Elcomsoft iOS Forensic Toolkit, Lantern, AccessData MPE+, iXAM, and XRY. For a more comprehensive and detailed list of tools, books, and papers related to physical acquisition, refer to *Appendix A, References*, and *Appendix B, Tools for iOS Forensics*.

Case study – physical acquisition with UFED Physical Analyzer

The physical acquisition in UFED Physical Analyzer can be started through the main interface of the software under the menu item, **Extract | iOS Device Extraction**, as follows:

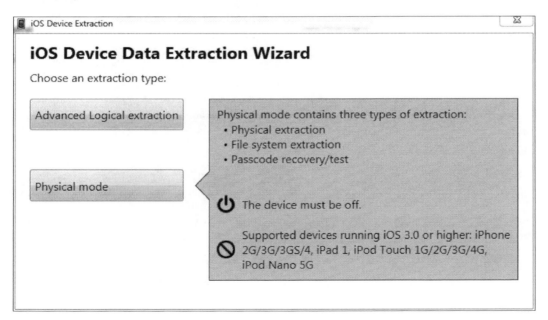

The device must be powered off and then the analyst can connect the correct cable to the computer (and not yet to the iDevice).

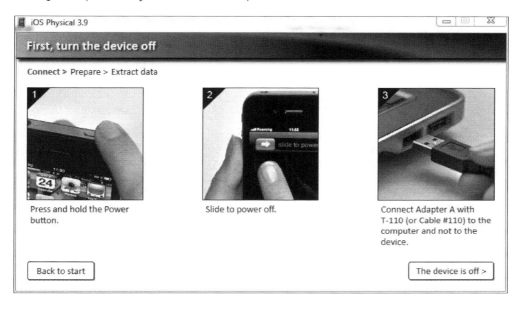

Now, the investigator must connect the device in **Recovery** mode. It means that they need to press and hold the Home button and connect the device, as shown in the following screenshot:

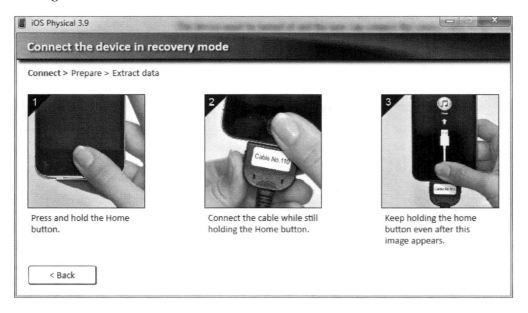

The software displays the information related to the device (the iOS version, serial number, board, boot firmware, chip ID, and so on), as follows:

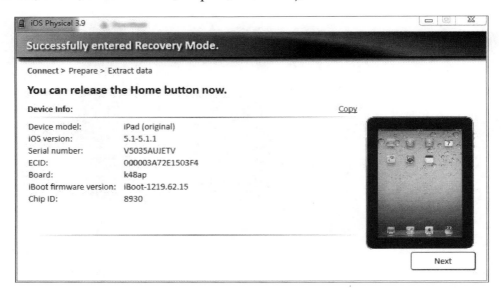

Now, the device must be set in **DFU** mode by pressing the Power and Home buttons together, and release the Power button 3 seconds after the device screen becomes black.

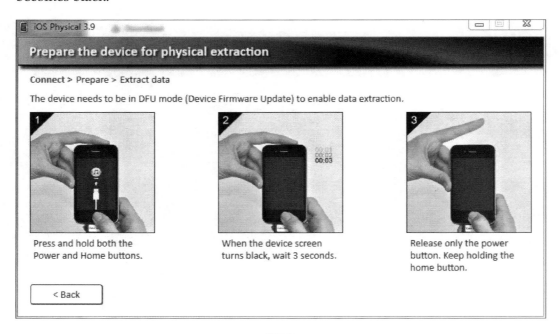

The software uploads in memory the boot loader and provides the analyst with two options: **Physical Extraction** and **File System Extraction,** as shown in the following screenshot. The first one extracts a physical image of the encrypted data partition, so the extraction can be viewed in UFED Physical Analyzer and in other analysis tools. UFED also provides information about the passcode protection. If the device is not protected by a passcode, it can start the acquisition immediately and decrypt all the files.

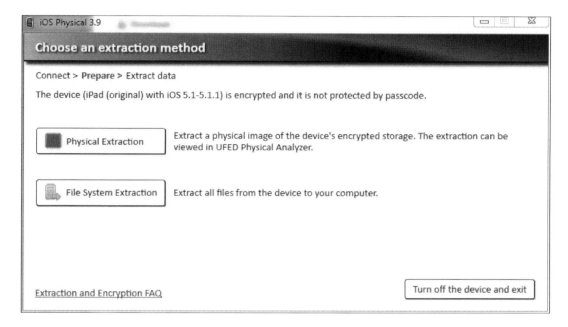

Otherwise, it depends by the passcode type. If the device has a simple passcode (4 digits), it can be cracked in 20 to 30 minutes (depending on the iDevice type) by choosing the **Passcode recovery** option.

The device (iPad (original) with iOS 5.1-5.1.1) is encrypted and protected with a simple passcode. All data can be fully extracted and decrypted in UFED Physical Analyzer. The passcode can be recovered automatically, if you don't know the passcode.

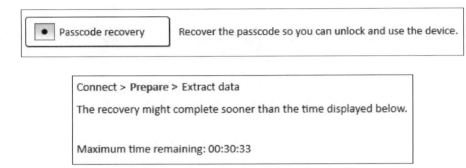

At the end of the cracking stage, the software shows the passcode and gives the opportunity to start the acquisition, as follows:

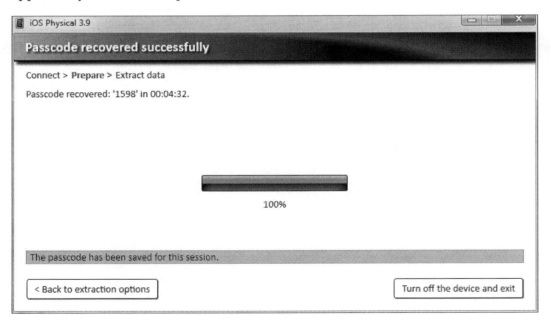

If the device has a complex passcode, the analyst has two options: acquire a physical image without cracking the passcode (this means that some data will not be available, for example, e-mail and stored password) or try to crack the passcode with a dictionary attack.

> The device (iPad (original) with iOS 5.1-5.1.1) is encrypted and protected with a complex passcode. All data can be fully extracted and decrypted if you have the passcode. Without the passcode, some files (such as part of the emails and saved passwords) will still be encrypted.

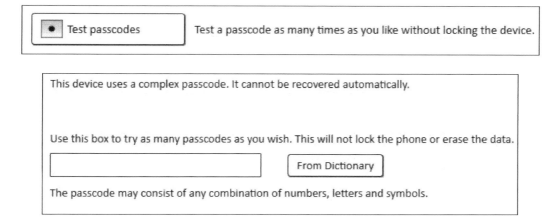

The iOS device jailbreaking

iOS jailbreaking is the process of removing limitations on the iOS devices through the use of software and hardware exploits. It enables root access to the iOS file system and allows additional applications not available in the official Apple App Store to be downloaded. Various jailbreaking tools have been developed; an always updated list can be found at http://theiphonewiki.com/wiki/Jailbreak. Currently, the latest available tools are **Evasi0n** (http://evasi0n.com/), **Pangu** (http://en.pangu.io/), and **Taig** (http://www.taig.com/en/).

Jailbreaking is an invasive activity on the device system partition, so it cannot be considered as a forensic operation. However, it is useful to note that for newer devices (iPhone 4s/5/5C, iPad 2/3/4/Mini, and iPod Touch 5), it is the only way to make a physical acquisition. It is therefore necessary that the device is already jailbroken or that the investigator can jailbreak it. On newer devices, in order to jailbreak the device, the analyst needs to know the passcode, since it requires actions to be performed directly on the unlocked device.

Case study – jailbreaking and physical acquisition with Elcomsoft iOS Forensic Toolkit

Only Elcomsoft iOS Forensic Toolkit supports the physical acquisition of new devices and it can be used on Windows or Mac. The following screenshots show the acquisition procedure performed on an iPad mini first generation device with passcode known and iOS 6.1.2.

The device was connected to a computer with Windows 7 operating system and jailbroken with evasi0n 1.5.3, as shown in the following screenshot. The step in which the software prompts you to unlock the device to complete jailbreaking should be noted.

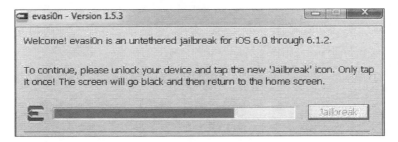

After jailbreaking, the software Elcomsoft iOS Forensic Toolkit for jailbroken devices was executed.

```
              Welcome to Elcomsoft iOS Forensic Toolkit
            This is driver script version 1.21/Win for A5+

                    (c) 2011-2013 Elcomsoft Co. Ltd.


Please select an action:
   1  N/A
   2  N/A
   3  GET PASSCODE     - Recover device passcode
   4  GET KEYS         - Extract device keys and keychain data
   5  DECRYPT KEYCHAIN
   6  IMAGE DISK       - Acquire physical image of the device filesystem
   7  DECRYPT DISK
   8  TAR FILES        - Acquire user's files from the device as a tarball
   9  REBOOT           - Reboot the device

   0  EXIT

>:
```

The wizard is very simple and basically involves the following three steps:

- Extraction of the encryption keys:

```
              Welcome to Elcomsoft iOS Forensic Toolkit
              This is driver script version 1.21/Win for A5+

                    (c) 2011-2013 Elcomsoft Co. Ltd.

Device keys file <keys.plist>:

Write decrypted image to file <keychain.txt>:
```

- Physical acquisition of the system partition (in plain text) and data partition (encrypted):

```
              Welcome to Elcomsoft iOS Forensic Toolkit
              This is driver script version 1.21/Win for A5+

                    (c) 2011-2013 Elcomsoft Co. Ltd.

Please select partition to image:
  1  System (rdisk0s1s1) -- this one is NOT ENCRYPTED
  2  User   (rdisk0s1s2) -- this one is ENCRYPTED

  0  Back

>:
```

```
Please select partition to image:
  1  System (rdisk0s1s1) -- this one is NOT ENCRYPTED
  2  User   (rdisk0s1s2) -- this one is ENCRYPTED

  0  Back

>: 2
Save image to file <user.dmg>:

rawwrite dd for windows version 0.6beta3.
Written by John Newbigin <jn@it.swin.edu.au>
This program is covered by terms of the GPL Version 2.

0k root@localhost's password:
14,393,856k
899616+0 records in
899616+0 records out
```

- Decryption of the data partition with the extracted keys:

```
                Welcome to Elcomsoft iOS Forensic Toolkit
                This is driver script version 1.21/Win for A5+

                    (c) 2011-2013 Elcomsoft Co. Ltd.

Encrypted image file <user.dmg>:
Device keys file <keys.plist>:
Write decrypted image to file <user-decrypted.dmg>:
```

```
                This is iOS User Partition Decryption Tool
                   Part of Elcomsoft iOS Forensic Toolkit
                    Version  1.15 built on Jun   4 2012

                    (c) 2011-2012 Elcomsoft Co. Ltd.

[INFO] Complete key set is loaded, everything should be decryptable.
[INFO] Image encryption statistics:
[INFO]   8141 files total: 7958 encrypted + 183 not encrypted.
[INFO]   7958 files can be decrypted (out of 7958 encrypted files).
[INFO] Input image contains 3598464 blocks of 4096 bytes.
[100%] 13.73 of 13.73 Gb decrypted
SHA1(user-decrypted.dmg) = 2168fc154d71feb4964d8cf0e4bf2bbb746c885a

Press 'Enter' to continue
```

Apple support for law enforcement

On a regular basis, Apple publishes a document on its website called *Legal Process Guidelines for U.S. Law Enforcement*. These guidelines contain information on how to request Apple support to recover information from iCloud or from an iDevice, and specify the data that Apple, in some cases, can extract from a passcode-protected device. Apple's latest available version states (https://www.apple.com/privacy/docs/legal-process-guidelines-us.pdf) that:

> "For all devices running iOS 8.0 and later versions, Apple will no longer be performing iOS data extractions as the data sought will be encrypted and Apple will not possess the encryption key. For iOS devices running iOS versions earlier than iOS 8.0, upon receipt of a valid search warrant issued upon a showing of probable cause, Apple can extract certain categories of active data from passcode locked iOS devices. Specifically, the user generated active files on an iOS device that are contained in Apple's native apps and for which the data is not encrypted using the passcode ("user generated active files"), can be extracted and provided to law enforcement on external media. Apple can perform this data extraction process on iOS devices running iOS 4 through iOS 7. Please note the only categories of user generated active files that can be provided to law enforcement, pursuant to a valid search warrant, are: SMS, iMessage, MMS, photos, videos, contacts, audio recording, and call history. Apple cannot provide: email, calendar entries, or any third-party app data."

This method was used, for example, by the South Africa police, who requested help to Apple in order to access data stored on Oscar Pistorious' iPhone.

Search and seizure flowchart

In the following diagram, we provide a flowchart useful during the search and seizure phase of iDevices. It illustrates the procedure to follow when an iDevice is found. In particular, it describes how to proceed if the iDevice is turned on or off and whether it is locked with a passcode.

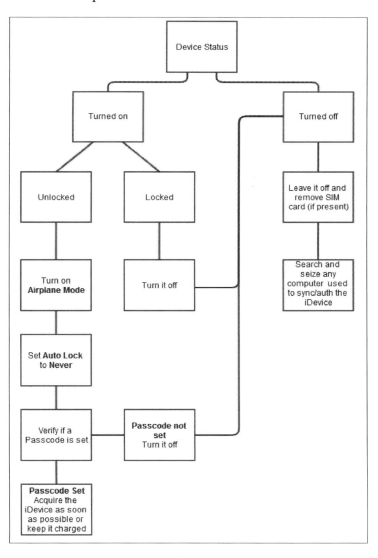

Extraction flowchart

In this section, we provide two flowcharts useful during the acquisition phase of iDevices.

The first flowchart illustrates the procedure to follow for old iDevices extraction (for example, iPhone 4, iPad 1, and so on) where physical acquisition is always possible.

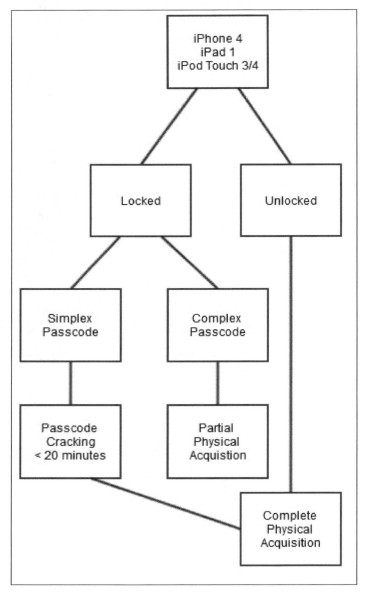

The second flowchart illustrates the procedure to follow for newer iDevices extraction (for example, iPhone 4s/5, iPad 2/3/4, and so on) where physical acquisition is not always possible.

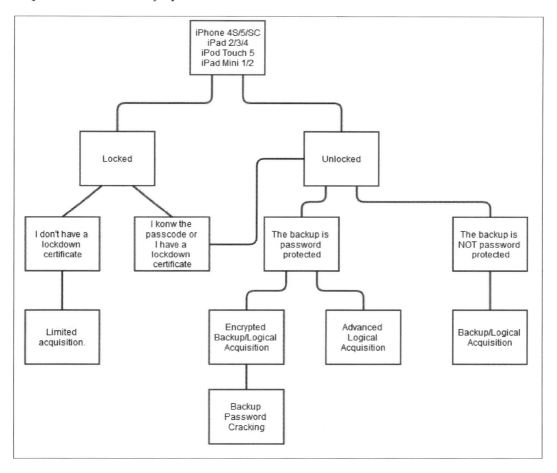

Summary

In this chapter, we introduced the four most-used methods to acquire data from iDevices: direct, backup or logical, advanced logical, and physical. The backup and logical acquisitions can be performed on any device but the device needs to be unlocked, or the analyst needs to know the passcode, or the analyst has a lockdown certificate extracted from a computer the device was previously synced with. If the user sets a password on the backup, the resulting acquisition is encrypted and so the analyst needs to try cracking the backup password (this topic is covered in detail in *Chapter 5, Evidence Acquisition and Analysis from iTunes Backup*). If the device is locked and the analyst doesn't know the code, or he/she doesn't have a lockdown certificate, only a very limited acquisition is possible: device name, device UDID, device Wi-Fi MAC address, and iOS version. The advanced logical acquisition can be performed with the same conditions of the backup or logical acquisition, but it can bypass the restrictions imposed by the backup password and extract the contents in clear text without the need to crack the backup password. The physical acquisition depends on the device and the operating system installed as follows:

- iPhone 2G/3G/3GS and iPod touch 1/2 with iOS 3 don't implement encryption and so it is always possible to perform a physical acquisition and the lock code can be cracked instantaneously. The resulting image is not encrypted. So, it is possible to carve deleted records.

- On iPhone 3GS/4, iPad 1, and iPod touch 3/4 with iOS 4/5/6/7, it is always possible to perform a physical acquisition. If the lock code is 4-digits long, it can be cracked in less than 20 minutes. So, it is possible to recover all the files. If a complex passcode is in use, the analyst can try to crack it with a brute force or dictionary attack. If it's not possible to crack it, it is possible to perform a physical acquisition and decode the file system (with the extracted file system key) and all the files whose encryption does not depend on passcode.

- On iPhone 4s/5/5C, iPad2, iPad mini 1, and iPod touch 5 with iOS 4/5/6/7, physical acquisition is possible only if the device is already jailbroken or if it is possible to jailbreak it (it means that the analyst must know the code).

- On iPhone 5s/6/6 Plus, iPad Air, and iPad mini 2, it is not possible currently to perform a physical acquisition although there are studies and researches on it.

In the next chapter, we will introduce you with the most interesting and useful artifacts that can be found on iDevices.

Self-test questions

1. How is the way in which iOS devices operate to upgrade the operating system called?

    1. Normal

    2. Recovery

    3. Device Firmware Upgrade

    4. Update

2. Where are the lockdown certificates stored in Windows 7/8?

    1. `C:\Program Data\Apple\Lockdown`

    2. `C:\Users\[username]\AppData\Roaming\Apple Computer\Lockdown`

    3. `C:\Users\[username]\AppData\Local\Apple Computer\Lockdown`

    4. `C:\Windows\Apple Computer\Lockdown`

3. Which of the following tools can be used to perform a physical acquisition of a jailbroken iPhone 4s?

    1. iOS Forensic Toolkit

    2. Oxygen Forensics Suite

    3. Cellebrite UFED Touch

    4. Mobile Phone Examiner

4. What is the latest iPhone model that can be physically acquired even if it is not jailbroken?

    1. iPhone 3GS

    2. iPhone 4

    3. iPhone 5

    4. iPhone 6

5. How is the device identifier for iOS devices called?

    1. ECID

    2. UDID

    3. Serial Number

    4. MAC Address

4
Analyzing iOS Devices

The goal of this chapter is to guide you to the analysis of important artifacts that are present on an iDevice. In the first part, the focus will be on the artifacts generated by the features of the system or by the interaction of the user with it, referring mainly to the iOS configuration files and to the iOS native applications. In the second part, we will go through the manual analysis of some of the most common third-party applications, with the goal of giving you a general approach that you will be able to apply to all the different apps you will encounter in your way. About this topic, there are also several publications available, some of which you will find the references in the *Appendix A, References*. We will conclude with a case study to provide you also with a proprietary analysis software example. All of this focusing on the two main formats used to store data: **SQLite** databases and **property list** (`plist`) files.

How data are stored

Before actually starting the analysis of the artifacts we can find inside an iDevice, let's take a look at how data are structured and in which format they are stored. Inside the Apple file system, most of the user data are stored under `/private/var/mobile/`, or simply `/User/` that is a symlink pointing to the previous directory:

```
# tree -d -L 2 /private/var/mobile/
/private/var/mobile/
|-- Applications
|    |-- 18073081-5AA9-4E02-B6B7-4AD8DAF7E677
|    |-- 1B880E57-314B-41E2-879E-189F423DBE05
|    |-- 22B5EA26-BD8A-4F53-8557-90656158B46E
...
|-- Containers
|-- Documents
```

```
|     `-- com.apple.springboard.settings
|-- Library
|     |-- Accounts
|     |-- AddressBook
|     |-- AggregateDictionary
...
|     |-- Inboxes
|     |-- Keyboard
|     |-- Logs
|     |-- Mail
...
|     |-- Preferences
|     |-- SMS
|     |-- Safari
...
|     |-- SoftwareUpdate
|     |-- Spotlight
|     |-- SpringBoard
...
|-- Media
|     |-- Airlock
|     |-- ApplicationArchives
|     |-- Books
|     |-- DCIM
|     |-- Downloads
...
`-- MobileSoftwareUpdate
```

While you may easily guess the meaning of most of the folders, you may wonder what those names inside the `Applications` folder are. These are the names of the apps represented by their **Universally Unique ID (UUID)**. Inside each application folder, you will see, most of the times, the same structure that looks something like this:

```
# tree -L 1 FAA3360F-18A5-4EA2-A331-53F2A49C5A8E/
FAA3360F-18A5-4EA2-A331-53F2A49C5A8E/
|-- Documents
|-- Library
```

```
|-- StoreKit
|-- Telegram.app
|-- iTunesArtwork
|-- iTunesMetadata.plist
`-- tmp
```

In particular:

- `/private/var/mobile/Application`: This path is the actual path where `/User/Application` also points to
- `/User/Applications/########-####-####-####-############`: In this path, the # symbols represent the UUID
- `<Application_Home>/AppName.app`: This file is the application bundle, which will not be backed up
- `<Application_Home>/Documents/`: This path contains application-specific data files
- `<Application_Home>/Library/`: This path contains application-specific files
- `<Application_Home>/Library/Preferences/`: This path contains application-preference files
- `<Application_Home>/Library/Caches/`: This path contains application-specific support files, which will not be backed up
- `<Application_Home>/tmp/`: This path contains temporary files not persistent between application launches, which will not be backed up.

It has to be noted that, however, these paths have slightly changed with the introduction of iOS 8. In fact, the path, /private/var/mobile/Application/, has been changed to /private/var/mobile/Containers/Bundle/Application/. Keep this in mind also for the other paths you will encounter in the rest of this book.

From the root application folder, the `iTunesMetadata.plist` contains, among others, information related to the product, the Apple account name, and the date of purchase, which may turn useful in some cases. You will find one of these files in each application directory.

▼ accountInfo		Dictionary	(12 items)
AccountURLBagType		String	production
CreditDisplayString		String	
AccountServiceTypes	⊕ ⊖	Number	0
DidFallbackToPassword		Boolean	NO
AccountStoreFront		String	143450~2,21 ab:XYZ1
AccountIsNewCustomer		Boolean	NO
AccountKind		Number	0
AccountAvailableServiceTypes		Number	0
AppleID		String	demo @gmail.com
AccountSocialEnabled		Boolean	NO
AccountSource		String	device
DSPersonID		Number	1.627.312.175
purchaseDate		String	2014-09-16T13:32:57Z

Regarding the format that Apple uses to store its files, you will encounter mostly two types: **plist**, mainly used for configuration files, and **SQLite databases**. We will look more into details about both formats in the next section.

Timestamps

A very important aspect that you have to pay attention to is the timestamp convention used. This is crucial especially if you are analyzing the artifacts manually without one of the specialized commercial tools. Instead of the classical **UNIX Epoch Time**, which represents the number of second elapsed since January 1, 1970 00:00:00, the iOS devices adopt the **MAC Absolute Time**, which represents the number of seconds elapsed since January 1, 2001 00:00:00. The difference between the two is 978,307,200 seconds. There are several resources available online that you could use to calculate it, or else you do it on your Mac by adding the preceding value to the MAC Absolute Time value, as in the following example:

```
$ date -u -r `echo '314335349 + 978307200' | bc`
Sat Dec 18 03:22:29 UTC 2010
```

 Remember to insert the –u switch in order to display it in UTC time or else the system will give you an output on your local time (or whatever is set as the local time in your machine).

Databases

The most common type of data storage on the iOS devices (just like on other mobile platforms in general) is the use of the SQLite databases. Both native as well as third-party applications heavily use SQLite database files to store their data, as we will see more in details later.

There are several tools available, both free/open source and commercial, such as *SQLite Database Browser* that offers a GUI interface, as well as the SQLite command-line utility, available from the official SQLite website, http://www.sqlite.org/. If you are using Mac OS X as machine for the analysis, it will come with the sqlite3 utility preinstalled.

The property list files

The property list files, or plist, are the other most common data formats used in the iOS devices (and in Mac OS X as well). The plist files are mainly used to store configuration information, preferences, and settings. Its format can be compared to the XML format and are usually represented as binary or plain text files.

A common tool used for parsing a plist file under Windows is *plist Editor Pro*, while if you are using Mac OS X you can either use XCode to view the plist files or the command-line utility, plutil.

The iOS configuration files

iOS has many preference and configuration files where it stores tons of data that may turn valuable during an investigation. This section wants to provide you with a detailed (although not exhaustive) list of some of those that are useful to keep in mind, as follows:

- **Account and device information**: Check out /private/var/root/Library/Lockdown/data_ark.plist. It contains various information about the device and about its account holder.

- **Account information**: Have a look at /private/var/mobile/Library/Accounts/Accounts3.sqlite. This file contains account information.

- **Account information**: Go to /private/var/mobile/Library/DataAccess/AccountInformation.plist. You'll find account information used to set up apps here.

- **Airplane Mode**: Check /private/var/root/Library/Preferences/com.apple.preferences.network.plist. This specifies whether **Airplane Mode** is presently enabled on the device.

- **Application installed list**: Now have a look at `/private/var/mobile/Library/Caches/com.apple.mobile.installation.plist`. It contains a list of all installed applications on the device and the file paths to each application. This is useful to map application GUIDs to specific apps.

- **AppStore settings**: Check `/private/var/mobile/Library/Preferences/com.apple.AppStore.plist`. It contains the last store search.

- **Configuration information and settings**: Go to `/private/var/mobile/Library/Preferences/`. It contains the `plist` files with the system configuration and the settings of the Apple apps.

- **Lockdown certificate info**: Navigate to `/private/var/root/Library/Lockdown/pair_records/`. It contains information about the lockdown/pairing certificates and also the computers the iOS device has been paired with.

- **Network information**: Go to `/private/var/preferences/SystemConfiguration/com.apple.network.identification.plist`. It contains a cache of the IP networking information as the previous network addresses, router addresses, and name servers used. A timestamp for each network is also provided.

- **Notification log**: Check out `/private/var/mobile/Library/BullitenBoard/ClearedSections.plist`. It's a log of cleared notifications.

- **Passwords**: Go to `/private/var/Keychains/`. It contains the password saved in iDevice.

- **SIM card info**: Now have a look at `/private/var/wireless/Library/Preferences/com.apple.commcenter.plist`. It contains the ICCID and IMSI of the SIM card last used in the device.

- **Springboard**: Go through `/private/var/mobile/Library/Preferences/com.apple.springboard.plist`. It contains the order of applications in each screen.

- **System Logs**: Check `/private/var/logs/`. This folder contains the iOS system logs.

- **Wi-Fi networks**: Now see `/private/var/preferences/SystemConfiguration/com.apple.wifi.plist`. It contains the list of the known Wi-Fi networks, the timestamp of last joined, and several other useful information. For more information on this and a deeper analysis, you can have a look at the article available at `http://articles.forensicfocus.com/2013/09/03/from-iphone-to-access-point/`.

Native iOS apps

iDevices come with some native applications already installed by Apple, such as Safari browser, e-mail client, calendar, and utilities linked to some basic phone functionalities, such as the Camera, Call History, or the SMS/iMessage. Most of the evidence produced by these native applications and functionalities are located, other than inside the application folders themselves, in the `Library` folder:

- `/private/var/mobile/Library/`: In case of physical acquisition or inside the device
- `Backup Service/mobile/Library/`: In case of File System acquisition
- `Library`: In case of logical acquisition

Here, we can find data related to communication, preferences, Internet history and cache, keyboard keystrokes, and much more. Other than the `Library` folder, the other very important location is the `Media` folder, `/private/var/mobile/Media/`, where user-created pictures and audio files are usually stored among other things.

Address book

As one could imagine, the `AddressBook` folder under `Library` refers to the information present in the Contact application related to the personal contacts and are stored in SQLite database format. There are two databases of interest: `AddressBook.sqlitedb` and `AddressBookImages.sqlitedb`.

`AddressBook.sqlitedb` contains the actual information saved for each contact, such as name, surname, phone number, e-mail address, and so on. In this database, the tables of interest containing the information mentioned are mainly `ABPerson` and `ABMultiValue`.

`AddressBookImages.sqlitedb` is the database containing the images that the user may have associated to given contact, which is basically the image appearing every time a call to that contact is made or received. The main table of interest in this database is `ABFullSizeImage`.

Audio recordings

The Voice Memos app, preinstalled on the iDevices, lets the user record voice memos. These memos are stored in `/private/var/mobile/Media/Recordings/`. Inside this folder, there is the `Recordings.db` database that contains information about each voice memo stored, such as the date, duration, memo name, and filename of the actual audio file, which is stored in the same folder.

Calendar

The Calendar application allows the user to manually create events, as well as sync them with other application, such as the related Mac OS X version of the app or other third-party applications and services. Such information is stored in two databases:

- /private/var/mobile/Library/Calendar/Calendar.sqlitedb
- /private/var/mobile/Library/Calendar/Extras.db

The Calendar.sqlitedb database contains basically all the information related to the events present in the calendar, while Extras.db contains other information such as the Calendar settings or extra details to alarms linked to certain calendar event.

```
# sqlite3 Extras.db
SQLite version 3.7.13
Enter ".help" for instructions
sqlite> .mode line
sqlite> .tables
ZALARM          ZSETTING        Z_METADATA      Z_PRIMARYKEY
sqlite> SELECT * FROM ZALARM;
                    Z_PK = 1
                   Z_ENT = 1
                   Z_OPT = 1
                ZALARMID = 1
                 ZALLDAY =
               ZENTITYID = 53
ZISDELAYEDPROXIMITYALARM =
       ZACKNOWLEDGEDDATE = 0
             ZENTITYDATE = 437137200
                ZFIRETIME = 437136300
         ZENTITYTIMEZONE = Europe/Rome
             ZEXTERNALID = 4E96BF04-97C1-4D43-A638-5B465815DA13
```

Call history

When we push the phone application icon, we see a lot of information, almost all coming from one database `/private/var/wireless/Library/CallHistory/call_history.db`. Here we can find tracks about incoming, outgoing and missed calls along with time and date they occurred and their duration. This database refers to both standard calls and FaceTime calls. As we can see in the following example, the table of interest is `call`:

```
# ls -l
-rw-r--r-- 1 _wireless _wireless 28672 Oct  9 11:26 call_history.db
# sqlite3 call_history.db
SQLite version 3.7.13
Enter ".help" for instructions
sqlite> .mode line
sqlite> .tables
_SqliteDatabaseProperties  call
sqlite> SELECT * FROM call;
...
           ROWID = 3
         address = 119
            date = 1411901516
        duration = 174
           flags = 1
              id = -1
            name =
    country_code = 230
    network_code = 01
            read = 1
        assisted = 0
  face_time_data =
 originalAddress =
        answered = 0
```

In iOS 8, the path has slightly changed to `/private/var/wireless/Library/CallHistoryDB/CallHistory.storedata`.

Still related to the phone application, there are two other important files to analyze. The path, `/private/var/mobile/Library/Preferences/com.apple.mobilephone.plist`, contains `DialerSavedNumber`, which is the last phone number manually entered into the dialer and actually dialed. The important thing to note here is that this value will remain even if the user will delete the last call placed from the call history list, which will of course be also deleted from the `call_history.db` database we have just analyzed. The second file that may also be of interest during an investigation is `/private/var/mobile/Library/Preferences/com.apple.mobilephone.speeddial.plist`, which contains the phone numbers added to the phone favorites list.

E-mail

Apple Mail client-related data is stored at `/private/var/mobile/Library/Mail/`, which contains databases storing the e-mail messages sent, received, and drafted, which are stored on the device, as well as a folder for each separate account (POP/IMAP) that has been configured within the Mail application. So, you may want to take a look at all the content you find in there. To give you an example, the folder content may look like the following command:

```
# ls -l
-rw-r--r-- 1 mobile mobile      42 Nov  9 13:07 AutoFetchEnabled
-rw-r--r-- 1 mobile mobile   69632 Nov  8 16:15 Content\ Index
-rw-r--r-- 1 mobile mobile  192512 Nov  8 16:15 Envelope\ Index
-rw-r--r-- 1 mobile mobile   32768 Nov  8 16:15 Envelope\ Index-shm
-rw-r--r-- 1 mobile mobile 1347272 Nov  9 13:08 Envelope\ Index-wal
drwx------ 3 mobile mobile     136 Aug 19 15:10 IMAP-
<account_username>\@gmail.com\@imap.gmail.com/
-rw-r--r-- 1 mobile mobile     395 Nov  8 16:15
MailboxCollections.plist
drwx------ 2 mobile mobile     102 Aug 19 15:11 Mailboxes/
-rw-r--r-- 1 mobile mobile 1638400 Sep 28 13:14 Protected\ Index
-rw-r--r-- 1 mobile mobile   32768 Nov  8 16:15 Protected\ Index-shm
-rw-r--r-- 1 mobile mobile 1236032 Nov  8 16:15 Protected\ Index-wal
-rw-r--r-- 1 mobile mobile    4096 Jul 31 17:51 Recents
-rw-r--r-- 1 mobile mobile   32768 Nov  8 16:15 Recents-shm
-rw-r--r-- 1 mobile mobile 1256632 Nov  9 13:08 Recents-wal
drwx------ 2 mobile mobile      68 Jul 28 17:11 Vault/
-rw-r--r-- 1 mobile mobile     333 Nov  9 13:08 metadata.plist
```

Although without any extension, most of these files are SQLite databases (as you may guess from the presence of the -shm and -wal files). For example, the Envelope Index database contains the list of mailboxes and metadata, while Protected Index database contains the list of the e-mails present in the Inbox, where the last is the most recent:

```
# sqlite3 Protected\ Index
SQLite version 3.7.13
Enter ".help" for instructions
sqlite> .mode line
sqlite> .tables
message_data   messages
sqlite> SELECT * FROM messages;
message_id = 9
    sender = "Facebook" <update@facebookmail.com>
   subject = You have more friends on Facebook than you think
       _to = Demo < <account_username>@gmail.com>
...
message_id = 130
    sender = "PayPal" <paypal@e.paypal.it>
   subject = Accordi legali PayPal
       _to = <account_username>@gmail.com
...
```

Images

User photos inside iDevice are stored at /private/var/mobile/Media/, where the two main folders are as follows:

- DCIM: This folder contains the user-created photos via the built-in camera (usually in the .jpg format) and screenshots taken by the user by pressing Power and Home buttons together (usually in the .png format)

- PhotoData: This folder contains, among other data, the photo albums synced with a computer or the cloud

Moreover, it is very important not to forget the *thumbnails*. In fact, for each photo, iOS will generate a thumbnail and store within /private/var/mobile/Media/PhotoData/Thumbnails/ and save any information about the original image in the Photos.sqlite database. This is important because thumbnails and information related to the original picture may still be available or recoverable from the SQLite deleted entries (see the related section later on this chapter) even in case the original picture is not available anymore.

For an in-depth analysis of this topic, we advise the reader to have a look at the article available at `http://linuxsleuthing.blogspot.it/2013/05/ios6-photo-streams-recover-deleted.html`.

Maps

Since the release of iOS 6 in 2012, Apple includes its own Maps application. Files and locations of interest are `/private/var/mobile/Library/Preferences/com.apple.Maps.plist`, which contains information related to the last search that has been made by the user, such as longitude and latitude coordinates as well as the search query made, and the Maps' main folder (`/private/var/mobile/Library/Maps`), which contains the history of the of the searches made by the users as well as the list of locations bookmarked:

```
# ls -l
-rw-r--r-- 1 mobile wheel   4954 Nov  9 14:05 Bookmarks.plist
-rw-r--r-- 1 mobile wheel      0 Nov  9 14:02 Bookmarks.synced
-rw-r--r-- 1 mobile mobile     0 Jul 28 17:13 FailedSearches.mapsdata
-rw-r--r-- 1 mobile wheel   5372 Nov  9 14:02 History.mapsdata
-rw-r--r-- 1 mobile wheel      0 Nov  9 14:02 History.synced
drwxr-xr-x 3 mobile mobile   102 Jul 28 17:13 ReportAProblem/
-rw-r--r-- 1 mobile mobile  4867 Nov  9 14:06 SearchResults.dat
```

Notes

The Notes application stores information about the user created notes in the `/private/var/mobile/Library/Notes/notes.sqlite`. The main tables of interest are ZNOTE and ZNOTEBODY; they contain note title, content, creation and modification date, and so on.

```
# sqlite3 notes.sqlite
SQLite version 3.7.13
Enter ".help" for instructions
sqlite> .mode line
sqlite> .tables
ZACCOUNT       ZNOTE           ZNOTECHANGE    ZSTORE        Z_PRIMARYKEY
ZNEXTID        ZNOTEBODY       ZPROPERTY      Z_METADATA
sqlite> SELECT * FROM ZNOTE;
...
```

```
             ZCREATIONDATE = 429638384.376295
         ZMODIFICATIONDATE = 437233446.565407
                   ZAUTHOR =
                     ZGUID =
                 ZSERVERID =
                  ZSUMMARY = This is extra text of my note
                    ZTITLE = ThisIsMyPasswordCopyPaste
...
sqlite> SELECT * FROM ZNOTEBODY;
                     Z_PK = 1
                    Z_ENT = 4
                    Z_OPT = 2
                   ZOWNER = 1
                 ZCONTENT = ThisIsMyPasswordCopyPaste<div><br></
div><div>This is extra text of my
note</div>
...
```

Safari

Safari is the Apple browser that comes preinstalled with every iDevice. It allows the user to browse websites, save bookmarks, and so on. All these activities are stored in the two locations, /private/var/mobile/Library/ and the Safari main application folder. In particular, the folder detail is given as follows:

- **Safari Bookmarks**: The information is stored at Library/Safari/ Bookmarks.db. It contains the database with the saved bookmarks.

- **Safari Bookmarks**: The information is stored at Library/Safari/ Bookmarks.plist.anchor.plist. Timestamp identifies the last time Safari bookmarks were modified.

- **Safari Cookies**: The information is stored at Library/Cookies/Cookies. binarycookies. Web sites cookies are stored here.

- **Safari Screenshots**: The information is stored at Library/Caches/Safari/. This directory contains thumbnails referring to screenshots of web pages that have been recently visited by the user.

- **Safari Search cache**: The information is stored at Library/Caches/Safari/ RecentSearches.plist. It contains the most recent searches that the user has entered into Safari's search bar.

- **Safari search history**: The information is stored at `Library/Preferences/com.apple.mobilesafari.plist`. It contains a list of recent searches made through Safari. An important thing to remember is that when the user deletes his/her browser cache or history, this file will not be erased.

- **Safari Suspended State**: The information is stored at `Library/Safari/SuspendState.plist`. It contains the last state of Safari at the time the user pressed the Home button, the iPhone was powered off, or the browser crashed. In order to be able to restore such state when the browser resumes, this file will contain the list of windows and websites that were open when one of the previously-mentioned events occurred and the browser closed.

- **Safari Thumbnails**: The information is stored at `Library/Caches/Safari/Thumbnails/`. This directory will contain screenshots of the last active browser pages viewed via WebKit, for example, by the third-party apps.

- **Safari Web Cache**: The information is stored at `Library/Caches/com.apple.mobilesafari/Cache.db`. It contains objects that are recently downloaded and cached in the Safari browser.

- **Safari History**: The information is stored at `Library/Safari/History.plist`. It contains the Safari web browser history. Of course, if it has been cleared by the user, it will not contain the history prior to that.

SMS/iMessage

Like for the Call History, there is one database storing SMSs, MMSs, and iMessages sent or received by the user. The database is at `/private/var/mobile/Library/SMS/sms.db`, and it contains also the information related to attachments eventually present in MMS or iMessages. In such case, the files part of MMSs or iMessages are stored in the subfolder, `Library/SMS/Attachments/`. Finally, the last folder of interest regarding SMS is `Library/SMS/Drafts`, where each draft contains its own folder as the `plist` file, which is time stamped identifying when the message was typed and then abandoned.

Voicemail

The `Voicemail` folder at `/private/var/mobile/Library/` contains both the audio file of each voicemail recorded message stored as AMR codec audio files and the `voicemail.db` database, where are saved information related to each voicemail audio message file, such as the sender, the date, the duration, and so on.

Other iOS forensics traces

In this section, we will list some other locations of interesting artifacts. Those listed here are not strictly related to a particular application but are rather generated from the usage of the device by the interaction of the user with the system.

Clipboard

The pasteboardDB file under /private/var/mobile/Library/Caches/com.apple. UIKit.pboard is a binary file that contains a cached copy of the data stored on the device's clipboard, which means that the data that have been cut/copied and pasted by the user (that is, passwords or other portions of text that may become relevant) will also be present there.

Keyboard

Two of the iOS features are the auto correction and auto completion of the text while the user is typing. To do this, every time the user types, iOS caches his/her text in the dynamic-text.dat file.

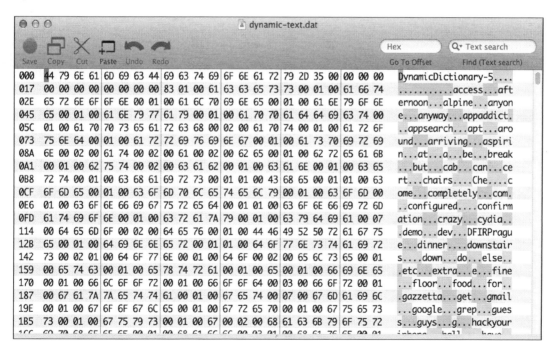

This file is located at /private/var/mobile/Library/Keyboard. This is the default file, but of course, iOS creates one for each language used and configured in the keyboard and stores it in the same directory. In the following example, the second file is related to the Italian keyboard configuration:

```
# ls -l
drwxr-xr-x 4 mobile mobile  136 Aug 14 15:48 CoreDataUbiquitySupport/
-rw------- 1 mobile wheel  1084 Nov  9 14:44 dynamic-text.dat
-rw------- 1 mobile wheel  6678 Nov  9 14:43 it_IT-dynamic-text.dat
```

Location

With iOS 4, there was the **Consolidated GPS cache**, a database containing location information associated with every Wi-Fi hotspot and cell tower that the device had been in range with. In such database located at /private/var/root/Library/Caches/locationd/consolidated.db, the WifiLocation and CellLocation tables contain information cached locally by the device and include the Wi-Fi access points and cellular towers that have come within range of the device at a given time and include a horizontal accuracy (in meters), believed to be a guestimate at the distance from the device. Such data, other than remaining forever in that database, were allegedly sent periodically to Apple. After the so-called **location gate** scandal that arose after the discovery of such database, Apple kind of dismissed it.

However, a new database took the place of the consolidated.db, that is, /private/var/root/Library/Caches/locationd/cache_encryptedA.db. As for its predecessor, this database contains geographical coordinates of Wi-Fi access points and, apparently, cell towers that have been in the range of the device. The only differences in this case are that this data lasts only for 8 days before being cleared out. In the following output, you can see the names of the tables within the database:

```
$ sqlite3 cache_encryptedA.db
SQLite version 3.8.4.3 2014-04-03 16:53:12
Enter ".help" for usage hints.
sqlite> .tables
AppHarvest                      CellLocationLocalBoxes_rowid
AppHarvestCounts                CellLocationLocalCounts
CdmaCellLocationHarvest         LocationHarvest
CdmaCellLocationHarvestCounts   LocationHarvestCounts
CellLocation                    LteCellLocationHarvest
CellLocationBoxes               LteCellLocationHarvestCounts
CellLocationBoxes_node          PassHarvest
```

`CellLocationBoxes_parent`	`PassHarvestCounts`
`CellLocationBoxes_rowid`	`TableInfo`
`CellLocationCounts`	`UnknownCellLocationHarvest`
`CellLocationHarvest`	`UnknownCellLocationHarvestCounts`
`CellLocationHarvestCounts`	`WifiLocation`
`CellLocationLocal`	`WifiLocationCounts`
`CellLocationLocalBoxes`	`WifiLocationHarvest`
`CellLocationLocalBoxes_node`	`WifiLocationHarvestCounts`
`CellLocationLocalBoxes_parent`	

The other very important point to keep in mind regarding the geolocation artifacts is that many other applications, especially third party like those about fitness that people may use to keep track of their path when running, may store geographical coordinates and related timestamps as well and in clear text.

Snapshots

Every time a user pushes the Home button to move from an application screen back to the desktop, iOS uses a **fade-out** effect for the transition between the two screens. To do so, iOS creates screenshots of the current screen and then applies the fade-out effect to that picture. These screenshots are stored in the following locations:

- `/private/var/mobile/Library/Caches/Snapshots/`
- `/private/var/mobile/Applications/<app_UUID>/Library/Caches/Snapshots/`

The first path refers to the pre-installed Apple applications, while the second is the path where to find the snapshots for each application. It is clear that this feature could be a goldmine of information. For example, there could be screenshots containing SMS or e-mail messages that are no longer available because they have been deleted.

 It is important to remember that only the last snapshot is taken for each application. Therefore, the analyst should interact and browse inside the device as little as possible in order not to overwrite and lose possible crucial evidence.

Spotlight

As for the Mac OS X, Spotlight is the indexing feature or iOS that assists the user when searching for something like applications, SMS, contacts, notes, and so on. Spotlight indexes and searches are stored in /private/var/mobile/Library/ Spotlight/, where there are two folders, one related to the SMS searches and the other is the general Spotlight utility.

Wallpaper

Current images used as wallpaper are stored in /private/var/mobile/Library/ SpringBoard/. There are two different images: HomeBackgroundThumbnail. jpg, which refers to the wallpaper when the device is unlocked, and LockBackgroundThumbnail.jpg, which refers to the wallpaper of the device when it is locked.

Third-party application analysis

In the previous paragraphs, we have seen where important artifacts related to the iOS system settings and preferences, native iOS applications, and device features are located. These are locations to be aware of, and it is important to know how to analyze them since they are common to all iDevices. Instead, in the following paragraphs, we are going to show you a practical analysis of some of the most-used third-party applications.

Skype

Skype is probably the most-known and used software for VoIP and chatting.

```
# tree -L 2 2C5328B1-44B1-4467-B3A4-DEBDFBEB78D4/

2C5328B1-44B1-4467-B3A4-DEBDFBEB78D4/
├── Documents
│   ├── skype-cache-501.<skype_username>.Favourites.plist
│   ├── skype-cache-501.<skype_username>.chat-946.plist
│   ├── skype-cache-501.<skype_username>.chat-meta-data-946.plist
│   ├── skype-cache-501.<skype_username>.contacts.plist
│   └── skype-cache-501.<skype_username>.conversations.plist
├── Library
│   ├── Application Support
│   ├── Caches
│   ├── Cookies
```

```
|    └── Preferences
├── Skype.app
...
├── StoreKit
|    └── receipt
...
```

Starting from the `Preferences` folder, we can find the first important information inside the `com.skype.skype.plist` file: the username, as shown in the following screenshot:

WebKitOfflineWebApplicationCacheEnabled	Boolean	YES
WebDatabaseDirectory	String	/var/mobile/Applications/2C5328B1-44B1-4467-B3A4-DEBDFBEB78D4/Library/Caches
lastLoggedInSkypeName	String	pa a
LocationManagerCountryCode	String	IT

However, the preceding screenshot shows only the last username that has logged in. If we want to know all the profiles that have been logged in from this device, we have to look for other folders under `Library/Application Support/Skype/`, where we will find one folder for each account logged in with that device.

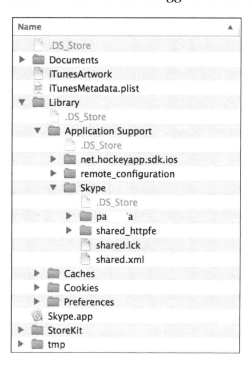

Inside every user folder we find all the databases storing information, such as contacts list, chats, and so on. Here, the structure is pretty much the same as the PC/desktop version. In fact, you can open the `main.db` file where you can find all information stored in clear, as you can see from the interesting names of the tables as follows:

```
# sqlite3 main.db
SQLite version 3.8.4.3 2014-04-03 16:53:12
Enter ".help" for usage hints.
sqlite> .tables
Accounts           ChatMembers      DbMeta           SMSes
Alerts             Chats            LegacyMessages   Transfers
AppSchemaVersion   ContactGroups    MediaDocuments   VideoMessages
CallMembers        Contacts         Messages         Videos
Calls              Conversations    Participants     Voicemails
```

Refer to the following screenshot:

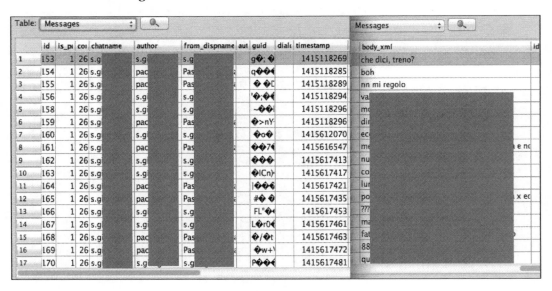

This means that you can use any of your favorite Skype analysis utilities to parse these files, such as **SkypeLogView** from **Nirsoft** and so on. Finally, still within the application folder, you may also find the Voicemail messages, screenshots, as we have addressed previously in the *Snapshots* section, files transferred via Skype, logs, and so on.

WhatsApp

Although it is technically an Instant Messaging application, WhatsApp has almost completely replaced the classical SMS. Therefore, it is very likely that you will encounter it during a mobile forensics analysis. Let's have a look at its internal directory structure that, as you may have realized, differs really very little from one application to the other.

```
# tree -L 2 7A2F36A2-7100-482C-B2E2-ED350D7BF0C2/
7A2F36A2-7100-482C-B2E2-ED350D7BF0C2/
├── Documents
│   ├── ChatSearch.sqlite
│   ├── ChatStorage.sqlite
│   ├── Colors.plist
│   ├── Contacts.sqlite
│   ├── PPDB.plist
│   ├── StatusList.plist
│   ├── SyncHistory.plist
│   ├── calls.backup.log
│   └── calls.log
├── Library
│   ├── Caches
│   ├── FieldStats
│   ├── Logs
│   ├── Media
│   ├── Preferences
│   └── pw.dat
├── StoreKit
│   └── receipt
├── WhatsApp.app
...
```

We have now understood that to get a first hint and useful information for starting with an application, we may want to start looking inside the `plist` configuration file under `Library/Preferences/`. In this case, we are looking for `net.whatsapp.WhatsApp.plist`. Here again, you will find some basic information, such as the username, the phone number the WhatsApp account was linked to, and so on. Regarding the actual content of the messages exchanged, the main database is `Documents/ChatStorage.sqlite`, whose structure is as follows:

```
$ sqlite3 ChatStorage.sqlite
SQLite version 3.8.4.3 2014-04-03 16:53:12
```

```
Enter ".help" for usage hints.
sqlite> .tables
ZWABLACKLISTITEM     ZWAGROUPINFO        ZWAMESSAGE         Z_METADATA
ZWACHATPROPERTIES    ZWAGROUPMEMBER      ZWAMESSAGEINFO     Z_PRIMARYKEY
ZWACHATSESSION       ZWAMEDIAITEM        ZWAMESSAGEWORD
```

The table ZWAMESSAGE is the one containing the messages exchanged, their timestamp, the name of who the user was chatting with, and so on, as shown in the following screenshot:

The ZWACHATSESSION table stores information about the open chats, both with a single user or group chats, and you can correlate these data with those in the ZWAGROUPMEMBER and ZWAGROUPINFO tables in order to find out which users belong to which group chat. Finally, in the ZWAMEDIAITEM are stored references to the multimedia files (pictures, audio messages, and videos) exchanged, indication of the user involved, timestamps, and the location where the multimedia file has been stored within iDevice.

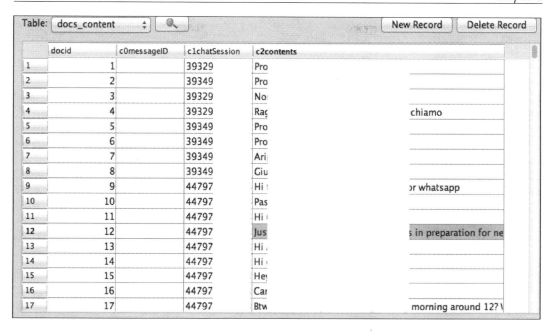

However you will also find the chat contents inside `Documents/ChatSearch.sqlite` within the `docs_content` tables, as shown in the preceding screenshot.

Facebook

Facebook is the most known and widely used social network. For this reason, other than for the fact that it is now integrated with iOS, you will most likely have to analyze the Facebook app in almost all of your investigations. As you can imagine, the amount of information stored by Facebook is very high, and in particular, it concerns three areas: user personal information, a cache of images related to profiles and visited pages, and information related to the external sites visited within the Facebook app through the links present on the posts. Due to the obvious big amount of possible information retrievable in the Facebook app and the page limitation of a book, the goal of this section is to give you a glimpse and some hints on possible artifacts and where to find them.

The account information is saved inside `Library/Preferences/com.facebook.plist`. Among other information, you will find the e-mail address and the Facebook ID of the profile configured within the app, as well as the date of the last time the app has been used.

Information related to contacts is saved in `Library/Caches/FbStore.db`, while the related profile pictures (the JPG file) are saved in the `Library/Caches/ImageCache/` folder.

In `Library/Caches/_store_<APP_ID>/<iOSVersion>_<language>/FBDiskCache/` are stored images viewed while surfing through the pages of the social network (for example, posts of other users and so on), while inside the database, `Library/Caches/com.facebook.Facebook/Cache.db`, and `Library/Caches/com.facebook.Facebook/fsCachedData/` are stored contents of other websites visited, including the related URL and corresponding files (for example, the JPG image, the HTML page, the CSS stylesheet, and so on.)

When the user watches a video within the social network, such information is stored in the database, `Library/Cache/com.facebook.Facebook/var/mobile/Applications/.../video_url_cache/Cache.db` and inside `Library/Cache/com.facebook.Facebook/var/mobile/Applications/.../video_url_cache/fsCachedData/`.

Cloud storage applications

Cloud storage applications have become very popular on mobile devices, since the Cloud somewhat extends the device storage capability and allows the user to have access to his/her data anywhere and anytime. Therefore, it is very probable that you will encounter at least one on this class of apps during your analysis. In this section, we just want to give you a glimpse of some artifacts you can find in two of the most popular cloud storage services.

Dropbox

The Dropbox iOS app is stored under `/private/var/mobile/Applications/4BD80D3B-7ADA-4171-B2A0-8A534F05408D/` and it contains four subfolders: `Cookies`, `DropboxPrivate`, `Preferences`, and `Cache`.

The `Cache` folder contains a local copy of the *opened files*, but it is *available only if we can perform a physical acquisition* (not logical/backup acquisition). The `Preferences` folder contains a file named `com.getdropbox.Dropbox.plist` with user information (name and surname) and user e-mail.

The following screenshot shows application structure and the user information in the `plist` file:

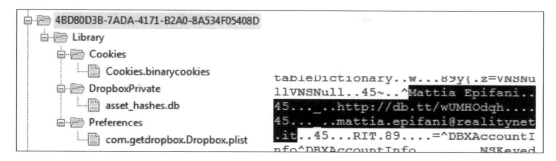

Google Drive

The Google Drive iOS App is stored in `/private/var/mobile/`
`Applications/8F139264-9142-4B84-A7C3-421ADD6BA05F/`, and it contains
two subfolders: `Documents` and `Library`, which in turns has the folders `Cookies`,
`Preferences`, and `Caches`. The `Preferences` folder contains a file named `com.`
`google.Drive.plist` with user information (name and surname), user ID, and user
e-mail, as shown in the following screenshot:

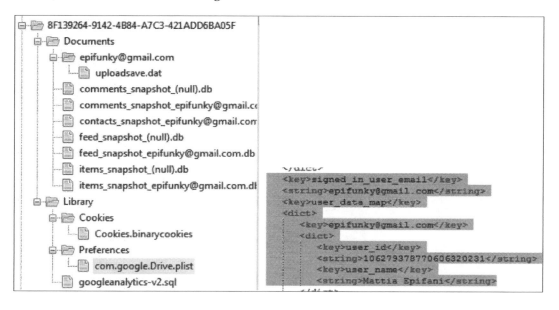

The `Caches` folder contains the *cached copy of the opened files*, but *it can be extracted only
if we can perform a physical dump.*

The `Documents` folder contains three interesting SQLite databases: `Contacts_snapshot_useremail.db`, `Feed_snapshot_useremail.db`, and `Items_snapshot_useremail.db`.

The Contacts db contains the user's e-mail ID, name, and shared files. The Items db contains all the information about files stored in the user drive:

- Identifier
- Title
- Kind
- MD5 hash
- Last Modified By (username)
- Last Modified Date
- Last Viewed Date
- Shared With Me Date
- Last Modified by Me Date

The following screenshot shows the Items db content analyzed with SQLite Expert for Windows:

title	kind	owner
		Click here to define a f
Electronic Evidence Guide	spreadsheet	epifunky@gmail.com
I miei file	folder	<null>
Electronic Evidence Guide.xlsx	application/vnd.openxmlformats-officedocument.spreadsheetml.sheet	epifunky@gmail.com
Data dell'evento di DFA	spreadsheet	epifunky@gmail.com

md5Checksum	last_modified_by	last_modified_date	last_viewed_date	shared_with_me_date	last_modified_by_me_date
ilter					
<null>	paolo	1374941933	1372929036	<null>	1372929293
<null>	<null>	<null>	<null>	<null>	<null>
fbcf7c391bc5832de7bc9408afaa27f0	epifunky	1371543822	<null>	<null>	1371543821
<null>	epifunky	1290425344	1347934116	<null>	1290425344

Deleted data recovery

In this section, we will give you a quick overview on the difficulties of performing file carving operations on an iOS device and will try to understand why and what are the possibilities. We will also see the particular case of recovering the SQLite deleted records.

File carving – is it feasible?

Apple uses a technology called **Data Protection** in order to further protect data stored in flash memory on iDevices. Every time a file is created, a new 256-bit *per-file key* is generated and it is used to encrypt the file content using AES encryption. The *per-file key* is then wrapped with one of the data protection class keys and then stored in the file's metadata, which are in turn encrypted with the file system key (the **EMF key**), which is generated from the unique hardware UID. The following diagram, which is taken directly from the Apple iOS Security official paper of October 2014 (see *Appendix A, References*), summarizes the entire process:

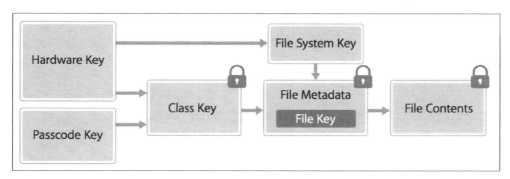

With this premise, it is clear that the classic file carving procedure will not work, since in the unallocated space there will only be encrypted content. An interesting approach on how to carve deleted images from the iOS devices has been published by D'Orazio et al. (see *Appendix A, References*). What they suggest is to exploit the journaling feature of the iOS file system, HFS+. In fact, by analyzing and comparing both the catalog file and the journal file of the HFS+ file system, it could be possible to identify information about deleted files, such as file and metadata location, their timestamp, and so on. Based on this information from the journal, the analyst should be able to search and recover the deleted files, locate the cryptography keys, and then decrypt the image file. Heather Mahalik (@HeatherMahalik on Twitter) also describes a similar approach in her book, *Practical Mobile Forensics, Heather Mahalik, Packt Publishing*. Of course, such approaches require physical acquisition to be possible for the target device.

However, that approach may work only if the device has not been restored, wiped, or upgraded to a new OS version, because in such cases, the file system key (EMF) would be erased and a new key recreated. Therefore, without the original EMF key, all contents in the unallocated space referring to a period prior the restoring/wiping/upgrading is gone forever.

Carving SQLite deleted records

We will not go into the details of the SQLite structure (for more information, see *Appendix A, References*), since it is out of the scope of this book. However, it is important for you to know that other than deleted files, it is also possible to recover deleted records within the SQLite databases. Mari DeGrazia (@maridegrazia on Twitter) has developed a useful Python script that parses the database file and carves out deleted entries. Its usage is as simple as running a single-line command as follows:

```
$ python sqlparse.py -f mmssms.db -r -o report.txt
```

You can find it on her website and GitHub repository; she has also provided a GUI version of the tool (see *Appendix A, References*, and *Appendix B, Tools for iOS Forensics*). Moreover, it is always useful to run a strings command on the database file as well. You may be able to recover portion of deleted entries content that may have been missed by the tools.

Case study – iOS analysis with Oxygen Forensics Suite 2014

The acquisition of an iPhone made with Oxygen Forensics Suite 2014 can be analyzed directly within the same tool. In fact, during the acquisition, all the files are parsed by the software, which offers the user a complete GUI to access and search for information in the data. The following screenshot used to show the different functionalities of the software, refers to a logical classic type of acquisition from an iPhone 4s with iOS 7.1.1. Some descriptions of the features of Oxygen Forensics Suite 2014 have been taken directly from the vendor website, http://www.oxygen-forensic.com.

The screen shown in the following screenshot summarizes the main information related to the acquired device: model, operating system version, serial number, acquisition type, extraction date, investigator name, case number, and evidence number.

Moreover there are also present two separate areas: the first one refers to **Common sections**, that is the information related to native applications and to the grouping functionalities offered by the software; the second one refers to the activities of the main applications installed on the device by the user.

The analysis of native applications lets the analyst recover much information, such as the phonebook with assigned photos, calendar events and notes, call log (facetime, dialed, received, and missed calls), messages (SMS/MMS and iMessages), and voicemail. The following screenshot shows an example of a call history:

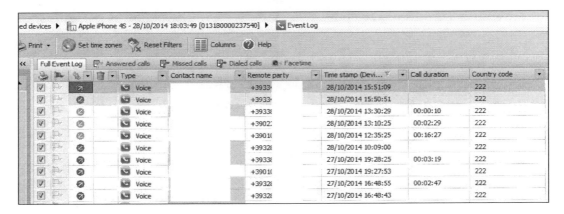

Moreover, with Oxygen Forensics Suite 2014, it is possible to recover information related to Wi-Fi access points, IP connections, and locations. The following screenshot shows the detail of Wi-Fi networks stored in the device under analysis. For each network, the SSID, MAC address of the router/access point, and the connection timestamps (last joined time and last auto joined time) are listed. From websites such as www.wigle.net, it is possible to trace the MAC addresses and find the physical position of where the device was.

Regarding the analysis of the applications installed by the user, the software extracts and interprets both databases and configuration files (usually in the `plist` format) for the most common applications present on the Apple Store. These applications are split in the following categories:

- **Messengers**: Facebook, Skype, WhatsApp, Viber, Telegram, Facebook Messenger, Yahoo, Google Hangouts, KiK Messenger, QQ, testPlus, Line, and so on

- **Navigations**: Google Maps, Apple Maps, Waze, and so on

- **Browser**: Safari, Google Chrome, and so on

- **Social networks**: Facebook, LinkedIn, Twitter, Instagram, Vkontakte, and so on

- **Travel**: Booking, SkyScanner, and so on

- **Productivity business**: Google Drive, Dropbox, and iBooks

The following screenshot shows an example of WhatsApp analysis:

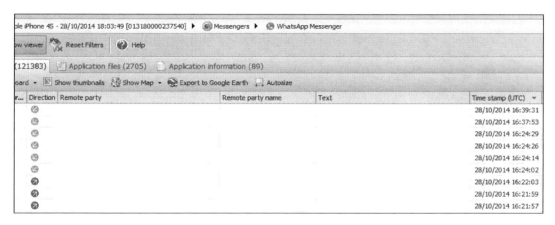

Finally, the software offers advanced functionalities for cross-searching data as follows:

- **Aggregated Contacts**: This section analyzes the contacts from multiple sources such as the Phonebook, Messages, Event Log, Skype, chat, and messaging applications in **Aggregated Contacts**. This section automatically reveals the same people in different sources and groups them in one meta-contact.

- **Dictionaries**: This section shows all the words ever entered in device messages, notes, and calendar.

- **Links and Stats**: This section reveals social connections between users of mobile devices under investigation and their contacts. The **Links and Stats** section provides a tool to explore social connections between device users by analyzing calls, text, multimedia and e-mail messages, and Skype activities.

- **Timeline**: This section organizes all calls, messages, calendar events, geo data and other activities in chronological way, so the analyst can follow the conversation history without the need to switch between different sections.

- **Social Graph**: This section is a workplace that allows the analyst to review connections between mobile device owners and their contacts, pinpoint connections between multiple device owners, and detect their common contacts.

Other than the automated analysis, it offers also the ability to navigate inside the file system and view all the different file types (documents, images, videos, and audio). There are also two embedded tools to view SQLite databases and `plist` files. The first one also offers the possibility to recover the deleted records from databases, giving therefore the possibility to retrieve calls, messages, photo thumbnails, contact photos, applications databases, and so on.

The use of this software has resulted to be very easy, also for the user not having high technical skills. It allows performing searches of keywords in a very intuitive way, also applying filters on every field of the application analyzed. Finally, it allows also exporting findings and it automatically generates a report in different formats (Word, Excel, PDF, HTML, and so on).

A detailed list of the feature available for the iOS devices can be found at `http://www.oxygen-forensic.com/en/features/analyst/applications` and at `http://www.oxygen-forensic.com/en/compare/devices/software-for-iphone`.

Summary

In this chapter, we showed how to approach the analysis of both native iOS applications that come with every iOS device, as well as third-party applications. We saw some of the most common applications, but the approach is the same for any other. It became also clear the importance of being able to parse the `plist` files and SQLite databases, and to carve out deleted records from latter, since these are the two main data structures an analyst will have to deal with in every analysis. Last but not least, this chapter provides you with a good amount of locations of interesting forensics artifacts, as well as of tools to analyze them. Remember that in-depth analysis, references, and tools are available at *Appendix A*, *References*, and *Appendix B*, *Tools for iOS Forensics*, while in *Appendix C*, *iOS 8 – What it Changes for Forensic Investigators*, you will find references to what has changed with the new iOS 8.

In *Chapter 5*, *Evidence Acquisition and Analysis from iTunes Backup*, we will see how to acquire and analyze forensics evidences in the case of an iTunes Backup.

Self-test questions

1. In which iOS folder is most of the information of interest saved?
    1. `/private/var/mobile`
    2. `/Users/mobile`
    3. `/private/var/user/mobile`
    4. `/private/user/mobile`

2. Which is the timestamp convention used in iOS?
    1. UNIX Epoch Time
    2. Apple Time
    3. Windows Time
    4. MAC Absolute Time

3. What does the file com.apple.mobile.installation.plist contain?
    1. Last store search
    2. IP networking information
    3. List of installed applications
    4. Password saved in the iDevice

4. In which file is the information related to the SIM card used in the iDevice stored?

    1. `ClearedSections.plist`

    2. `com.apple.network.identification.plist`

    3. `com.apple.commcenter.plist`

    4. `com.apple.springboard.plist`

5. What is the name of the database containing the user address book?

    1. `AddressBook.db`

    2. `AddressBook.sqlitedb`

    3. `AddressBook.sqlite`

    4. `AB.db`

6. In which folder is the call history saved?

    1. `/private/var/CallHistory`

    2. `/private/var/wireless/Library/CallHistory/`

    3. `/private/var/Library/CallHistory/wireless`

    4. `/private/var/Library/CallHistory/`

7. What kind of file is used to store Safari browsing history?

    1. SQLite

    2. Txt

    3. Plist

    4. HTML

8. How is the file containing the keyboard cache used for auto correction and auto completion called?

    1. `UserDictionary.txt`

    2. `Dict.dat`

    3. `Dynamic-Text.dat`

    4. `Text.dat`

5
Evidence Acquisition and Analysis from iTunes Backup

The goal of this chapter is to introduce you to the different types of backups (encrypted or unencrypted) to the structure of a backup, to the techniques and software available to extract meaningful data from it, and to show you how to crack an encrypted backup while extracting the password saved into it. These concepts are really useful because sometimes the analyst doesn't have the iOS device or cannot access it, but he may have access to a computer containing an iTunes backup.

iTunes backup

The Apple iTunes software allows the user to create two different types of backup of their iOS devices: encrypted and unencrypted. An unencrypted backup is completely accessible, while an encrypted one is protected with a password chosen by the owner of the device. The first time that user sets a password for the backup, this is saved inside iDevice, and every subsequent backup is encrypted with the same password (until the user decides to change it). For this reason, if a password has already been set when performing a forensic acquisition, we would get an encrypted backup (see *Chapter 3, Evidence acquisition from iDevices*, for the different techniques used to acquire a device with a backup password set).

iTunes backup folders

The folder where the backup data is stored depends on your computer's operating system. iTunes saves the backup files in these folders:

- **Mac**: `~/Library/Application Support/MobileSync/Backup/`
- **Windows XP**: `\Documents and Settings\(username)\Application Data\Apple Computer\MobileSync\Backup\`
- **Windows Vista, Windows 7, and Windows 8**: `\Users\(username)\AppData\Roaming\Apple Computer\MobileSync\Backup\`

Inside these folders, there is a subfolder for each iDevice that has backup with the same computer. The name of the subfolder is equivalent to the UDID of the device, which is a 40 character long hexadecimal string. This means that iTunes holds only one backup for each device and copies only the files that have been modified since the last backup. When a device is updated to a new OS version and then restored, the last backup created before the update is not overwritten the first time you create a new backup. In particular, the old backup folder is renamed by appending the timestamp of the backup at the end of the folder name.

iTunes backup content

According to Apple specifications (see the article available at `http://support.apple.com/kb/ht4946`, as mentioned in *Appendix A, References*) inside a backup, we can find the following contents:

- Camera Roll (photos, screenshots, images saved, and videos taken)

  For devices without a camera, Camera Roll is called Saved Photos

- Contacts and Contact Favorites
- Calendar accounts and subscribed calendars
- Calendar events
- Safari bookmarks, cookies, history, offline data, and currently open pages
- Autofill for webpages
- Offline web app cache/database
- Notes
- Mail accounts (mail messages aren't backed up)
- Microsoft Exchange account configurations
- Call history

- Messages (iMessage and carrier SMS or MMS pictures and videos)
- Voicemail token
- Voice memos
- Network settings (saved Wi-Fi hotspots, VPN settings, and network preferences)
- Keychain (includes e-mail account passwords, Wi-Fi passwords, and passwords you enter into websites and some apps)
- App Store app data (except the app itself, its tmp, and the Caches folder)
- App settings, preferences, and data, including documents
- In-app purchases
- Game Center account
- Wallpapers
- Location service preferences for apps and websites you've allowed to use your location
- Home screen arrangement
- Installed profiles
- Map bookmarks, recent searches, and the current location displayed in Maps
- Nike + iPod saved workouts and settings
- Paired Bluetooth devices
- Keyboard shortcuts and saved suggestion corrections
- Trusted hosts that have certificates and can't be verified
- Web clips

One of the main differences between an unencrypted backup and an encrypted one is related to the Keychain file. Inside an unencrypted backup, this file is saved encrypted with a key that depends on the device's UID, and therefore, cannot be cracked offline neither reactivated on a different device from the one used to generate the backup. Instead in an encrypted backup, the Keychain file is encrypted with the backup password. This can be technically explained as follows:

- If the device does not have a backup password set by the user, *when performing the acquisition, it is possible to create an encrypted backup choosing a known password, and later being able to access the passwords saved in the keychain without the need of cracking anything*

- If the device has a backup password set by the user, when performing the acquisition, it is possible to create an encrypted backup, and then trying to crack the password in order to extract those saved in the keychain

In particular, the `Keychain` file contains the following types of password:

- Passwords of the Wi-Fi networks the device has been connected to
- Passwords of the e-mail accounts configured in Apple Mail
- VPN credentials
- Credentials of all third-party apps that use keychain as the password container

iTunes backup structure

In a backup folder, there are some standard files with fixed names and contents and hundreds of files with long hashed filenames consisting of 40 hex characters. The file name acts like a unique identifier for every file copied from iDevice. In fact, each file is named as the result of a SHA-1 hash calculated on the original full name of the file in the following form:

`Domain-[subdomain-]fullpath/filename.ext`

Consider the following example:

`AppDomain-com.skype.skype-Library/Preferences/com.skype.skype.plist`

Here, `AppDomain` is the name of domain, `Com.skype.skype` is the subdomain, and `Library/Preferences/com.skype.skype.plist` is the path and the name of file.

Calculating SHA-1 hash for `AppDomain-com.skype.skype-Library/Preferences/com.skype.skype.plist` gives us `bc0e135b1c68521fa4710e3edadd6e74364fc50a`.

This is actually the 40 character long string we're talking about in the context.

The meaning of the elements named domain and subdomain is explained later in this chapter.

Standard backup files

These files are created by the backup service and store information about the backup itself. The most useful files are as follows:

- Info.plist: This file is a plist file in plain text and stores data about the backed up device (such as date of backup creation, phone number, device name, GUID, ICCID, IMEI, product type, iOS version, serial numbers, UDID, and so on) and the iTunes software used to create the backup (iTunes version number and iTunes settings).

Root	dict	
Backup Path	string	C:\Users\Mattia.Mattia-PC\AppData\Roaming\Apple (
Build Version	string	11D167
Contains Application Data	boolean	true
Device Name	string	EpiPhone
Display Name	string	EpiPhone
GUID	string	7CF569633A914265E62A165A10EA82F2
ICCID	string	8939992280168824935
IMEI	string	013180000237540
Installed Applications	array	
Is Encrypted	boolean	false
Last Backup Date	date	2014-06-22T14:30:20Z
Phone Number	string	+39 334 2340899
Product Name	string	iPhone 4S
Product Type	string	iPhone4,1
Product Version	string	7.1.1
Serial Number	string	DNRJ9Z9SDTC0
Source Identifier	string	26ccdbcb74b2ab8e9e97aa096883a10442c6f2ef
Target Identifier	string	26ccdbcb74b2ab8e9e97aa096883a10442c6f2ef
Target Type	string	Device
Unique Identifier	string	26CCDBCB74B2AB8E9E97AA096883A10442C6F2EF
iBooks Data 2	data	...
iTunes Files	dict	
iTunes Settings	dict	
iTunes Version	string	11.1.5

- `Manifest.plist`: This file is a `plist` file and it describes the content of the backup. Inside this file, we can find the list of applications installed on the backed up device. For every application, there is the name and the particular version. Inside the file, there is also the date the backup was made, the backup type (encrypted versus unencrypted), and some information about iDevice and the iTunes software used.

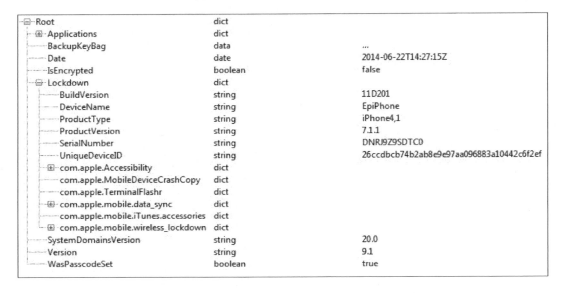

Root	dict	
Applications	dict	
BackupKeyBag	data	...
Date	date	2014-06-22T14:27:15Z
IsEncrypted	boolean	false
Lockdown	dict	
BuildVersion	string	11D201
DeviceName	string	EpiPhone
ProductType	string	iPhone4,1
ProductVersion	string	7.1.1
SerialNumber	string	DNRJ9Z9SDTC0
UniqueDeviceID	string	26ccdbcb74b2ab8e9e97aa096883a10442c6f2ef
com.apple.Accessibility	dict	
com.apple.MobileDeviceCrashCopy	dict	
com.apple.TerminalFlashr	dict	
com.apple.mobile.data_sync	dict	
com.apple.mobile.iTunes.accessories	dict	
com.apple.mobile.wireless_lockdown	dict	
SystemDomainsVersion	string	20.0
Version	string	9.1
WasPasscodeSet	boolean	true

- `Status.plist`: This file is a `plist` file in the binary format, and it stores information about the status of completion of the backup, whether the backup was made successfully or not.

- `Manifest.mbdb`: This file is a binary file that stores the descriptions of all the other files in the backup directory. It contains a record for each element in the backup (comprising symbolic link and directories, which of course don't have a corresponding element among the backup files). Each record contains the following parameters:

  ○ **Domain**: This parameter shows the domain the element belongs to. Domains are a way to functionally categorize elements in the device backup.

  ○ **Path**: This parameter shows the full path of the element.

  ○ **Link Target**: This parameter shows the target of the element if the element itself is a symbolic link.

- ° **User ID and Group ID**
- ° **m. time**: This parameter shows the time (in the Unix time format) when the actual content of the file was last modified.
- ° **a. time**: This parameter shows the time when the file was last accessed.
- ° **c. time**: This parameter shows the time when changes were last made to the file or to the directory's node.
- ° **File size**: This parameter shows the size of the file in bytes.
- ° **Unix file permissions**
- ° **File hash**

A really interesting thing to note from a forensics point of view is that *these four files are stored unencrypted also if the backup is encrypted with password*. It means that the information contained there is accessible also without cracking the password. For a detailed explanation of the analysis of an encrypted backup, we suggest the reading of the research made by Hal Pomeranz (see *Appendix A, References*). The preceding parameters are explained in the following diagram:

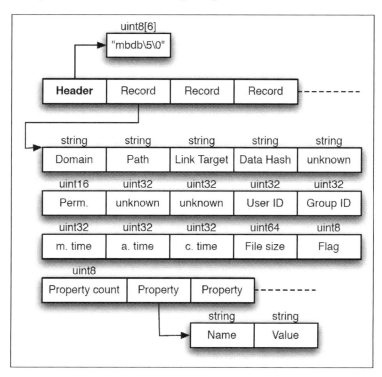

The first level of the hierarchy of the backup files is their domain. The domain for each file is written in its corresponding record in the `Manifest.mbdb` file. Each file has a domain name chosen from the following list:

- **App domain**: This domain contains data related to the installed apps
- **Camera Roll domain**: This domain contains multimedia elements related to the Camera application, such as images, videos, video previews, and image thumbnails
- **Home domain**: This domain contains data related to the standard application that comes preinstalled with iOS
- **Keychain domain**: This domain contains encrypted data related to the keychain
- **Managed Preferences domain**
- **Media domain**: This domain contains multimedia elements not related to the Camera application, such as multimedia elements from MMSs and audio recordings
- **Mobile Device domain**: This domain contains the provisioning profiles
- **Root domain**: This domain contains cache data related to the geolocation capabilities of the device
- **System Preferences domain**: This domain contains configuration files for core components of iOS
- **Wireless domain**: This domain contains data about the mobile phone component of the device

Elements in the App domain are further divided in subdomains related to the applications they belong to, while elements in the other domains don't use this feature. When the subdomain is used, the domain string is written as `<domain>-<subdomain>`. Details about the backup structure are available at https://theiphonewiki.com/wiki/ITunes_Backup.

iTunes backup data extraction

There are several tools available to extract data from an iTunes backup some open source software as well as commercial products. These tools allow you to have complete access to the data in case of unencrypted backup and partial access in case of an encrypted one (particularly, the content of the files will not be visible unless you know the backup password or you have been able to crack it). Among the most interesting and powerful tools for accessing and extracting data from backup there are forensic software (UFED Physical Analyzer, Oxygen Forensic® Suite , AccessData MPE+, EnCase, Elcomsoft Phone Viewer, and so on), commercial software for the data extraction (iBackup Bot, iPhone Backup Extractor, DiskAid, Wondershare Dr. Fone, and so on), and freeware/open source software for the data extraction (iPhone Backup Analyzer, iPhone Analyzer). A detailed list is provided in *Appendix B, Tools for iOS Forensics*. Another option is to recover the backup content on your own simply with an hex editor. In this case, we suggest you to read the article available at `http://resources.infosecinstitute.com/ios-5-backups-part-1/`.

Case study – iTunes backup analysis with iPBA

iPhone Backup Analyzer is a tool developed by the Italian researcher Mario Piccinelli and provides a simple way to browse through the backup folder and perform a forensic analysis of an iDevice backup. It is released as open source software under the MIT license and it is written in Python, and so it should be cross platform (Mac, Linux, and Windows).

The main goal behind the development is to provide a way to analyze the contents of the iPhone backup. It is meant to be used by anyone who wants to easily study what the backup contains, being a forensics expert, an iOS developer, or just an interested iPhone user. The software is also packed with utilities to easily browse through the content formatted in a ready-to-use way, such as messages, contacts, Safari bookmarks, and so on. Its complete feature set can be summarized in the following diagram:

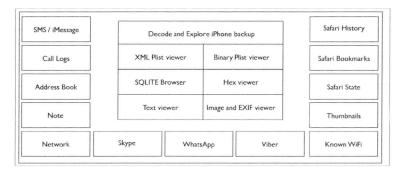

In a Windows environment, after downloading the tool, you need to unzip it to a folder and launch the executable `iPBA2.exe` file. By navigating to **File | Open Archive**, you can choose the folder containing the backup. The software parses and analyses the backup and provides a graphical way to browse through it.

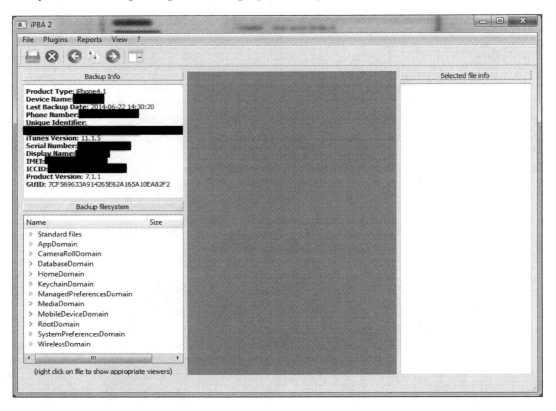

By right clicking on a `plist` or SQLite file, the analyst can view the file content. For example, in the following screenshot, you can see the content of the `Manifest.plist` file:

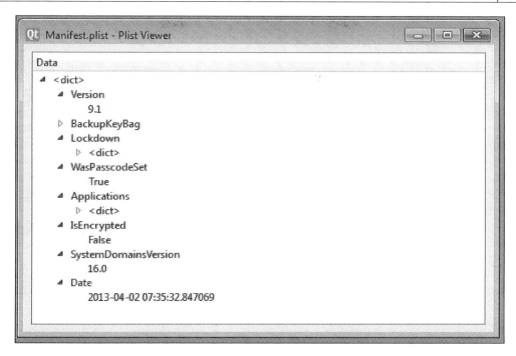

In the following screenshot, you can see the content of a Call History SQLite database:

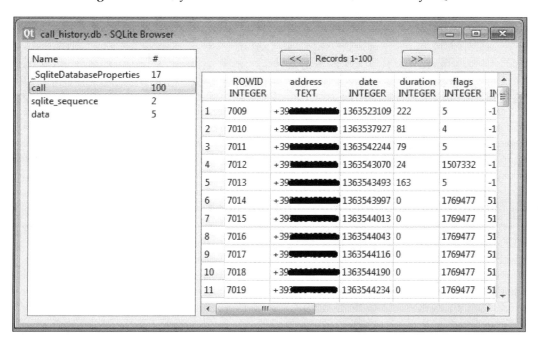

By choosing an item from the **Plugins** menu, you can also analyze useful information from the backup. Currently, the software offers 14 plugins: **Address Book Browser, Call History, Phone Info Browser, Known Networks, Network Identification, Note Browser, Safari History Browser, Safari State Explorer, Safari Bookmarks, Skype Browser, Messages Browser, Thumbnails Browser, Viber Browser**, and **WhatsApp Browser**. In the following screenshot, you can see, for example, the known Wi-Fi networks plugin:

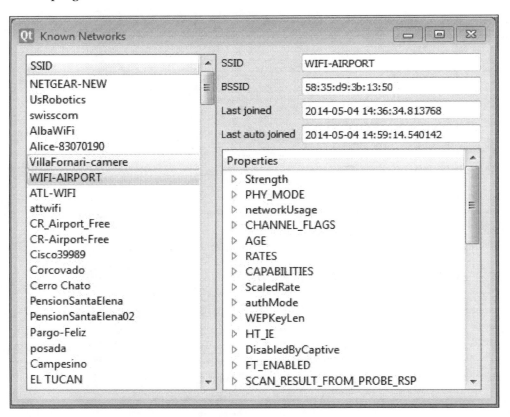

Encrypted iTunes backup cracking

As we explained in *Chapter 3, Evidence Acquisition from iDevices*, and in the first part of this chapter, an iTunes backup can be encrypted with a password chosen by the iDevice user. When you seize iDevice with a backup password already set or if you have a computer with a previously created encrypted backup, you can try to crack the backup using a dedicated tool. Currently, we were able to find only three software packages that can be used to crack an encrypted backup: EPPB, Passware Forensic, and iPhone Backup Unlocker.

Case study – iTunes encrypted backup cracking with EPPB

As from the product website, Elcomsoft Phone Password Breaker enables forensic access to password-protected backups for smartphones and portable devices based on the Apple iOS platforms. The password recovery tool supports Apple devices running iOS, including iPhone, iPad, and iPod touch devices of all generations released to date, including the iPhone 5s and iOS 7.

After launching the tool, the first step is to load the encrypted backup by clicking on the **Choose source** option from the main window and selecting **iOS device backup**, as shown in the following screenshot:

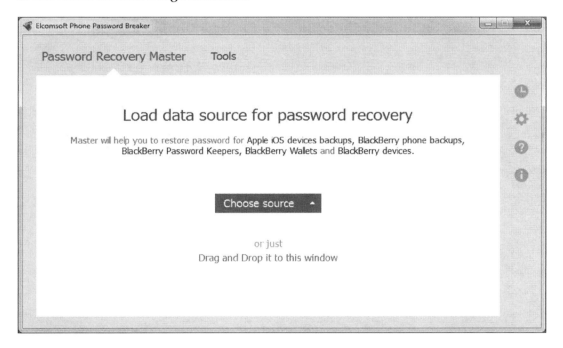

The software automatically provides a list of the encrypted backup saved in the folder of the user who is executing the tool.

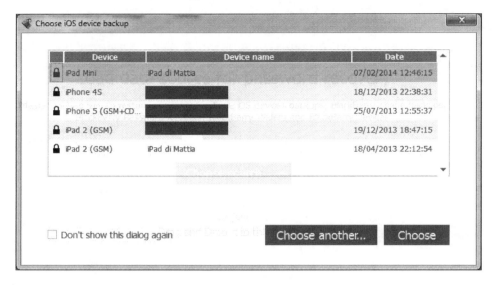

The analyst can choose one of the proposed encrypted backups or choose another folder containing other encrypted backups. After selecting the backup, the tool asks the analyst to select the type of cracking he/she wants to perform. You can choose between two options: **Dictionary Attack** or **Brute-Force Attack**, as shown in the following screenshot:

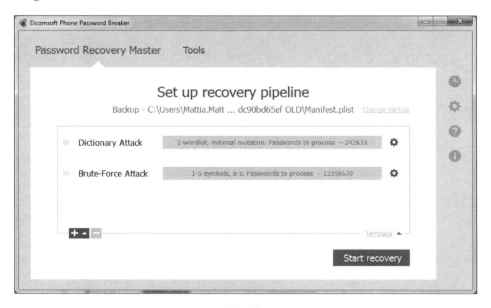

In the first case, the analyst can provide a custom dictionary file, as shown in the following screenshot:

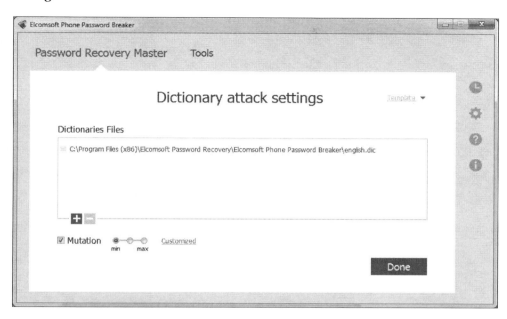

In the second case, the analyst can decide the parameters for the brute force attack, as follows:

If the cracking procedure is successful, the tool provides the password to the analyst and gives the options to *decrypt the backup* (so that it can be analyzed with one of the tools previously mentioned).

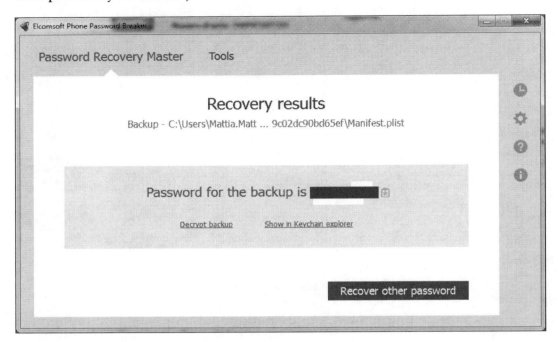

Otherwise, it is possible to show the keychain content with username and password for the Wi-Fi network connection, e-mail accounts configured in the Mail app, stored Internet passwords, and stored passwords from other apps.

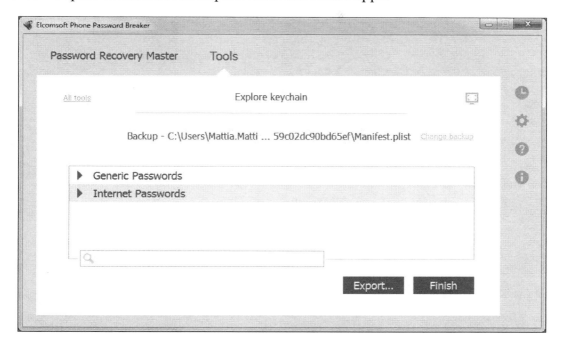

Summary

In this chapter, we explained the most useful information about iTunes backup related to the forensic analysis of an iOS device. In particular, we illustrated how the backup is structured and how to parse it with commercial and open source tools. We also explained the differences between an unencrypted and encrypted backup and suggested some ways to try to crack the backup password. A really interesting point about the iTunes backup is that if the device does not have a backup password already set by its owner, when preforming the acquisition, you can create an encrypted backup choosing a known password in order to be able to access the password saved in the `Keychain` file without the need of cracking. Instead, if you happen to have an encrypted backup for which you are not able to crack the password, it is anyway possible to analyze the `plist` files and the content of the `Manifest.mbdb` file recovering in this way the list of all files present inside that backup. In the next chapter, it will be explained how to recover data from the user iCloud account both having credentials or authentication token.

Self-test questions

1. In which folder are the iOS devices backup stored in Windows 7?

    1. `C:\Users\[username]\AppData\Roaming\Apple Computer\MobileSync\Backup`
    2. `C:\Users\[username]\AppData\Local\Apple Computer\MobileSync\Backup`
    3. `C:\Users\[username]\AppData\Apple Computer\MobileSync\Backup`
    4. `C:\Program Data\Apple Computer\MobileSync\Backup`

2. Which file contains information about the backup (such as backup date, device name, etc.)?

    1. `Manifest.plist`
    2. `Info.plist`
    3. `Status.plist`
    4. `Manifest.mbdb`

3. Which file contains the description of all the files in the backup directory?

    1. `Manifest.plist`
    2. `Info.plist`
    3. `Status.plist`
    4. `Manifest.mbdb`

4. Which backup domain contains multimedia elements related to the camera?

    1. App Domain
    2. Camera Roll Domain
    3. Media Domain
    4. Keychain Domain

6

Evidence Acquisition and Analysis from iCloud

The goal of this chapter is to introduce the cloud system provided by Apple to all its users through which they can save their backups and other files on remote servers. In the first part of the chapter, we will show you the main characteristics of such a service and then the techniques to create and recover a backup from iCloud.

iCloud

iCloud is a free cloud storage and cloud computing service designed by Apple to replace MobileMe. The service allows users to store data (music, pictures, videos, and applications) on remote servers and share them on devices with iOS 5 or later operating systems, on Apple computers running OS X Lion or later, or on a PC with Windows Vista or later. Similar to its predecessor, MobileMe, iCloud allows users to synchronize data between devices (e-mail, contacts, calendars, bookmarks, notes, reminders, iWork documents, and so on), or to make a backup of an iOS device (iPhone, iPad, or iPod touch) on remote servers rather than using iTunes and your local computer.

The iCloud service was announced on June 6, 2011 during the Apple Worldwide Developers Conference but became operational to the public from October 12, 2011. The MobileMe service was disabled as a result on June 30, 2012 and all users were transferred to the new environment. In July 2013, iCloud had more than 320 million users. Each iCloud account has 5 GB of free storage for the owners of iDevice with iOS 5 or later and Mac users with Lion or later. Purchases made through iTunes (music, apps, videos, movies, and so on) are not calculated in the count of the occupied space and can be stored in iCloud and downloaded on all devices associated with the Apple ID of the user. Moreover, the user has the option to purchase additional storage in denominations of 20, 200, 500, or 1,000 GB. Access to the iCloud service can be made through integrated applications on devices such as iDevice and Mac computers. Also, to synchronize data on a PC, you need to install the **iCloud Control Panel** application, which can be downloaded for free from the Apple website. To synchronize contacts, e-mails, and appointments in the calendar on the PC, the user must have Microsoft Outlook 2007 or 2010, while for the synchronization of bookmarks they need Internet Explorer 9 or Safari.

iDevice backup on iCloud

iCloud allows users to make online backups of iDevices so that they will be able to restore their data even on a different iDevice (for example, in case of replacement of devices). The choice of which backup mode to use can be done directly in the settings of the device or through iTunes when the device is connected to the PC or Mac, as follows:

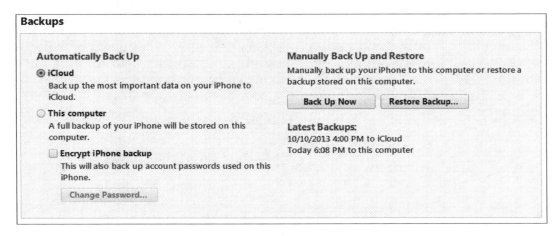

Once the user has activated the service, the device automatically backs up every time the following scenarios occur:

- It is connected to the power cable
- It is connected to a Wi-Fi network
- Its screen is locked

iCloud online backups are incremental through subsequent snapshots and each snapshot is the current status of the device at the time of its creation. The structure of the backup stored on iCloud is entirely analogous to that of the backup made with iTunes.

iDevice backup acquisition

Backups that are made online are, to all intents and purposes, not encrypted. Technically, they are encrypted, but the encryption key is stored with the encrypted files. This choice was made by Apple in order for users to be able to restore the backup on a different device than the one that created it. Currently, the acquisition of the iCloud backup is supported by two types of commercial software (**Elcomsoft Phone Password Breaker** (**EPPB**) and Wondershare Dr.Fone) and one open source tool (iLoot, which is available at `https://github.com/hackappcom/iloot`). The interesting aspect is that the same technique was used in the iCloud hack performed in 2014, when personal photos and videos were hacked from the respective iCloud services and released over the Internet (more information is available at `http://en.wikipedia.org/wiki/2014_celebrity_photo_hack`). Though there is no such strong evidence yet that describes how the hack was made, it is believed that Apple's *Find my iPhone* service was responsible for this and Apple did not implement any security measure to lockdown account after a particular number of wrong login attempts, which directly arises the possibility of exploitation (brute force, in this case). The tool used to brute force the iCloud password, named iBrute, is still available at `https://github.com/hackappcom/ibrute`, but has not been working since January 2015.

Case study – iDevice backup acquisition and EPPB with usernames and passwords

As reported on the software manufacturer's website, EPPB allows the acquisition of data stored on a backup online. Moreover, online backups can be acquired without having the original iOS device in hand. All that's needed to access online backups stored in the cloud service are the original user's credentials, including their Apple ID, accompanied with the corresponding password.

The login credentials in iCloud can be retrieved as follows:

- Using social engineering techniques
- From a PC (or a Mac) on which they are stored:
  - iTunes Password Decryptor (http://securityxploded.com/)
  - WebBrowserPassView (http://www.nirsoft.net/)

- Directly from the device (iPhone/iPad/iPod touch) by extracting the credentials stored in the keychain, as explained in *Chapter 5, Evidence Acquisition and Analysis from iTunes Backup*

Once credentials have been extracted, the download of the backup is very simple. Follow the step-by-step instructions provided in the program by entering username and password in **Download backup from iCloud** dialog by going to **Tools | Apple | Download backup from iCloud | Password** and clicking on **Sign in**, as shown in the following screenshot:

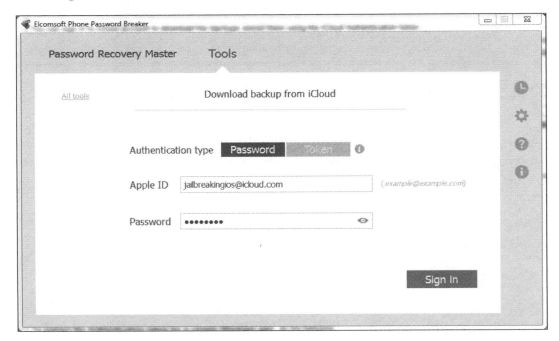

At this point, the software displays a screen that shows all the backups present in the user account and allows you to download data.

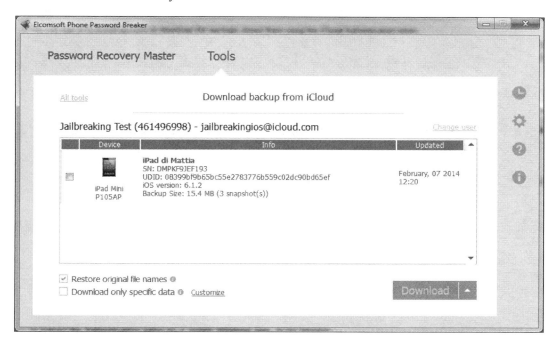

It is important to notice the possibility of using the following two options:

- **Restore original file names**: If enabled, this option interprets the contents of the `Manifest.mbdb` file, rebuilding the backup with the same tree structure into domains and sub-domains, as described in *Chapter 5, Evidence Acquisition and Analysis from iTunes Backup*. If the investigator intends to carry out the analysis with traditional software for data extraction from backups, it is recommended that you disable this option because, if enabled, that software will no longer be able to parse the backup.

- **Download only specific data**: This option is very useful when the investigator needs to download only some specific information. Currently, the software supports **Call history**, **Messages**, **Attachments**, **Contacts**, **Safari data**, **Google data**, **Calendar**, **Notes**, **Info & Settings**, **Camera Roll**, **Social Communications**, and so on. In this case, the **Restore original file names** option is automatically activated and it cannot be disabled.

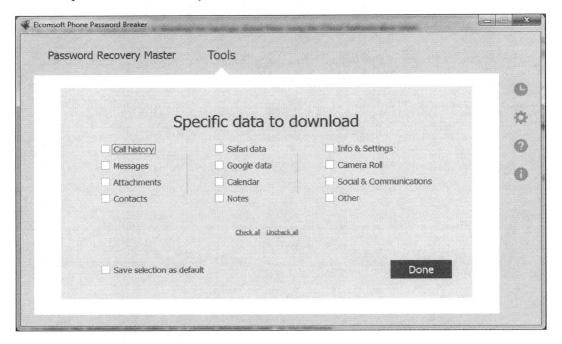

Once you have chosen the destination folder for the download, the backup starts. The time required to download depends on the size of the storage space available to the user and the number of snapshots stored within that space.

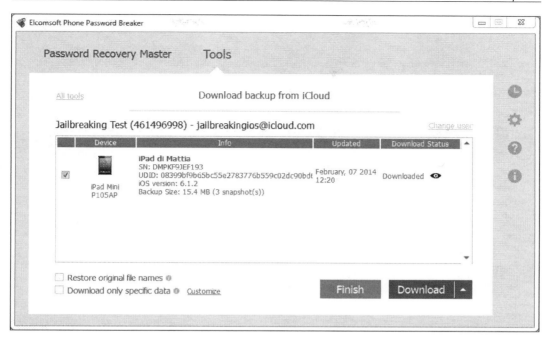

Case study – iDevice backup acquisition and EPPB with authentication token

The Forensic edition of Phone Password Breaker from Elcomsoft is a tool that gives a digital forensics examiner the power to obtain iCloud data without having the original Apple ID and password. This kind of access is made possible via the use of an authentication token extracted from the user's computer. These tokens can be obtained from any suspect's computer where iCloud Control Panel is installed. In order to obtain the token, the user must have been logged in to iCloud Control Panel on that PC at the time of acquisition, so it means that the acquisition can be performed only in a live environment or in a virtualized image of the suspect computer connected to Internet. More information about this tool is available at http://www.elcomsoft.com/eppb.html.

To extract the authentication token from the iCloud Control Panel, the analyst needs to use a small executable file on the machine called atex.exe. The executable file can be launched from an external pen drive during a live forensics activity.

Open Command Prompt and launch the `atex -l` command to list all the local iCloud users as follows:

Then, launch `atex.exe` again with the `getToken` parameter (`-t`) and enter the username of the specific local Windows user and the password for this user's Windows account.

A file called `icloud_token_<timestamp>.txt` will be created in the directory from which `atex.exe` was launched.

The file contains the Apple ID of the current iCloud Control Panel user and its authentication token.

Now that the analyst has the authentication token, they can start the EPPB software and navigate to **Tools | Apple | Download backup from iCloud | Token** and copy and paste the token (be careful to copy the entire second row from the .txt file created by the atex.exe tool) into the software and click on **Sign in**, as shown in the following screenshot. At this point, the software shows the screen for downloading the iCloud backups stored within the iCloud space of the user, in a similar way as you provide a username and password.

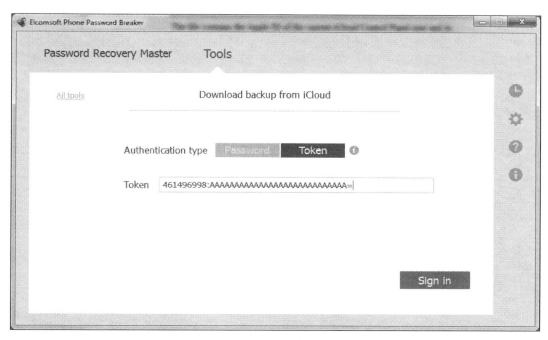

The procedure for the Mac OS X version is exactly the same. Just launch the atex Mac version from a shell and follow the steps shown previously in the Windows environment:

- `sudo atex -l`: This command is used to get the list of all iCloud users.
- `sudo atex -t -u <username>`: This command is used to get the authentication token for a specific user. You will need to enter the user's system password when prompted.

Case study – iDevice backup acquisition with iLoot

The same activity can be performed using the open source tool called iLoot (available at `https://github.com/hackappcom/iloot`). It requires Python and some dependencies. We suggest checking out the website for the latest version and requirements.

By accessing the help (`iloot.py -h`), we can see the various available options. We can choose the output folder if we want to download one specified snapshot, if we want the backup being downloaded in original iTunes format or with the Domain-style directories, if we want to download only specific information (for example, call history, SMS, photos, and so on), or only a specific domain, as follows:

```
Amministratore: C:\Windows\System32\cmd.exe

D:\Mattia\Download\iloot-master>iloot.py -h
usage: iloot [-h] [--output OUTPUT] [--combined] [--snapshot SNAPSHOT]
             [--itunes-style] [--item-types ITEM_TYPES [ITEM_TYPES ...]]
             [--domain DOMAIN]
             apple_id password

positional arguments:
  apple_id              Apple ID
  password              Password

optional arguments:
  -h, --help            show this help message and exit
  --output OUTPUT, -o OUTPUT
                        Output Directory
  --combined            Do not separate each snapshot into its own folder
  --snapshot SNAPSHOT   Only download data the snapshot with the specified ID.
                        Negative numbers will indicate relative position from
                        newest backup, with -1 being the newest, -2 second,
                        etc.
  --itunes-style        Save the files in a flat iTunes-style backup, with
                        mangled names
  --item-types ITEM_TYPES [ITEM_TYPES ...], -t ITEM_TYPES [ITEM_TYPES ...]
                        Only download the specified item types. Options
                        include address_book, calendar, sms, call_history,
                        voicemails, movies and photos. E.g., --types sms
                        voicemail
  --domain DOMAIN, -d DOMAIN
                        Limit files to those within a specific application
                        domain

D:\Mattia\Download\iloot-master>
```

To download the backup, you just only need to insert the account credentials, as shown in the following screenshot:

```
Amministratore: C:\Windows\System32\cmd.exe

D:\Mattia\Download\iloot-master>iloot.py username@icloud.com password
```

At the end of the process, you will find the backup in the output folder (the default folder's name is /output).

iCloud Control Panel artifacts on the computer

The installation of the iCloud Control Panel software, other than allowing the recovery of the user's authentication token, as shown previously, leaves logs of interest within the disk of the computer. On a Windows Vista/7/8 system, the logs of the connections to the iCloud service are stored inside C:\Users\<username>\ AppData\Roaming\Apple Computer\Logs. To locate logs of interest, it is necessary to search within the text file logs related to the executable iCloud.exe file. The files are named according to a standard format that includes the date and time at which the service has started (for example, asl.104019_04Oct12.log), thus letting the analyst to create a timeline of iCloud usage.

On a Mac OS X system instead, you will find plenty of the asl logs (the Apple system logs), so in order to check a user's iCloud activity, you will have to parse the following log files:

- /private/var/log/asl/YYYY.MM.DD.UID.asl
- /private/var/log/system.log

The user information configured in the iCloud Control Panel software is stored in the following file:

- **Windows**: C:\Users\<username>\AppData\Roaming\Apple Computer\ Preferences\mobilemeaccounts.plist
- **Mac OS X Mavericks**: Users/<user>/Library/Preferences/ MobileMeAccounts.plist

In particular, there is the following user information in the file:

- AccountDSID: This key denotes user identification
- AccountID: This key denotes the iCloud account username
- DisplayName: This key denotes the displayed name set by account owner
- IsPaidAccount: This key is set to True if the user has purchased additional services from Apple (more storage on iCloud)

- `LoggedIn`: This key denotes whether the user is automatically logged in or not in the service

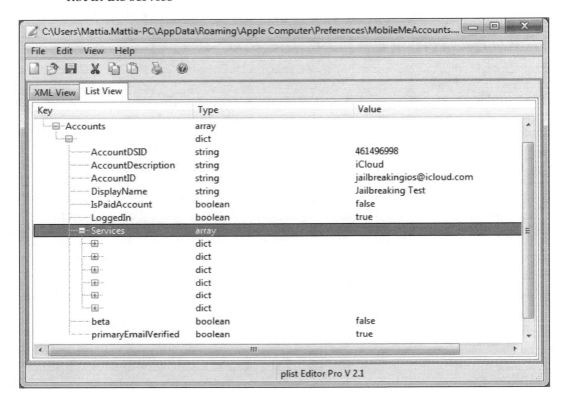

Summary

In this chapter, we introduced the iCloud service provided by Apple to store files on remote servers and backup their iDevice devices. In particular, we showed the techniques to download the backups stored on iCloud when you know the user credentials (Apple ID and password) and when you have access to a computer where it is installed and use the iCloud Control Panel software. In the next chapter, the application and malware analysis will be covered by providing an introduction to the tools and techniques most used for that kind of activity.

Self-test questions

1. When is a new backup on iCloud automatically created?

    1. Every 5 minutes
    2. It depends on the iOS version
    3. When the device is connected to the power cable, to a Wi-Fi network and is locked
    4. When the device is locked

2. Which of these tools can be used to download a backup from iCloud?

    1. iPhone Backup Analyzer
    2. iLoot
    3. UFED Physical Analyzer
    4. iOS Forensic Toolkit

3. Which tool can be used to recover the auth token from a PC with iCloud Control Panel?

    1. `Oauth.exe`
    2. `Iloot.exe`
    3. `Token.exe`
    4. `Atex.exe`

4. Where are the log files related to iCloud Control Panel stored in Windows 7?

    1. `C:\Users\[username]\AppData\Local\Apple Computer\Logs`
    2. `C:\Users\[username]\AppData\Local\Apple\Logs`
    3. `C:\Users\[username]\AppData\Roaming\Apple Computer\Logs`
    4. `C:\Users\[username]\AppData\Roaming\Apple \Logs`

7
Applications and Malware Analysis

Although malware for iOS devices is not so common, it is more common when considering jailbroken devices. As a forensic analyst, you may be required to analyze a malicious application, or more in general the behavior of a suspicious application you have never seen before. While we are not trying to write a comprehensive guide to static reverse engineering iOS applications, this chapter gives an overview of how to analyze an application, whether it is malicious or not. In this chapter, you will first learn how to set up the working environment, install, and configure the basic tools needed for iOS application analysis. Then, we will move the application analysis principles, learning at which state data can exist and where to look for them. Finally, we will see some tools in action that can help to speed up the analysis and automate some tasks.

Setting up the environment

The first step to take in order to properly set up a testing environment for iOS application analysis is to jailbreak your testing device. This is because, as an analyst, you need to have full control of what is happening in the device, being able to access all kinds of information, whether they are stored, in the memory, or being sent over the network.

How to jailbreak an iPhone is out of the scope of this book, so we will not go into details on how to do it; it is also quite simple. Just download one of the software options available, such as Evasi0n (advised), Redsn0w, or Pangu, and follow the instructions.

Once the device has been jailbroken and Cydia installed, you also need to install these tools:

- **OpenSSH**: This tool will allow you to log in to your jailbroken device via Wi-Fi or USB and have a root shell access into it
- **MobileTerminal**: This tool will allow you to run terminal commands on your device directly from your device, rather than logging in via ssh from a different system
- **BigBoss recommended tools**: This package contains a series of useful command-line tools such as apt, make, wget, sqlite3, and so on

Something you will always need to do when analyzing a malicious application is interacting with your iPhone via shell, whether to install new tools or launch specific commands from the shell; this is why we installed OpenSSH. The first thing you need to do is to change your default root password, which is alpine, in order to prevent someone else logging remotely into your device (and with root privileges!). To do this, launch the MobileTerminal application you just installed and run the following commands:

```
# su root
Password:
# passwd
Changing password for root.
New password:
Retype new password:
#
```

Now, there is a nice and comfortable way to connect to your iPhone via USB instead of being obliged to go over Wi-Fi. In your computer, edit the ~/.ssh/config file by adding the following entry:

```
Host usb
HostName 127.0.0.1
Port 2222
User root
RemoteForward 8080 127.0.0.1:8080
```

This will map the usb hostname to the ssh connection with the proper parameters needed. Moreover, the last row sets up port forwarding such that any connections to port 8080 on the iPhone will be forwarded to port 8080 locally on the laptop. This will be useful when you have to set up a proxy to intercept the network communications, as you will see later in this chapter. Now, you need something listening on port 2222: usbmuxd. This daemon is in charge of multiplexing connections over USB to the iDevice. To complete the procedure on OSX, you can simply use the following command:

```
$ brew install usbmuxd
$ iproxy 2222 22
$ ssh usb
```

Done! Now, you have a shell in your iPhone via USB.

Before installing the other tools, it is a good practice to make sure the baseline is up to date. To do this, just execute the following command from your root shell:

```
# apt-get update
# apt-get upgrade
```

The update command gets the latest packages list from the default repository, while the upgrade command will fetch the new versions of packages that already exist on the device and don't have the latest version installed using the information received by the update command run before.

The class-dump-z tool

The class-dump-z command is a command-line tool used to extract the Objective-C class information from the iOS applications. To install the tool, go to its official web page (https://code.google.com/p/networkpx/wiki/class_dump_z) and copy the link address of the last version, which currently is 0.2a. Then, using SSH, get into your device, fetch it with wget in a folder of your choice, and then extract it as follows:

```
# mkdir mytools
# cd mytools
# wget http://networkpx.googlecode.com/files/class-dump-z_0.2a.tar.gz
...
# tar xvzf class-dump-z_0.2a.tar.gz
```

Once done, open the `iphone_armv6` folder and copy the `class-dump-z` command executable in `/usr/bin` so that you will be able to run it from anywhere inside your iPhone. Then, just type `class-dump-z` to verify if it has been successfully installed as follows:

```
# cd iphone_armv6/
# cp class-dump-z /usr/bin/.
# cd ~
# class-dump-z
Usage: class-dump-z [<options>] <filename>
where options are:

  Analysis:
    -p          Convert undeclared getters and setters into properties
(propertize).
    -h proto    Hide methods which already appears in an adopted
protocol.
    -h super    Hide inherited methods.
    -y <root>   Choose the sysroot. Default to the path of latest
iPhoneOS SDK, or /.
    -u <arch>   Choose a specific architecture in a fat binary (e.g.
armv6, armv7, etc.)
```

However, beware that `class-dump-z` is not compatible with 64-bit architectures, which means from iPhone 5s on. In that case, you may want to have a look at the other tool, `class-dump`, available on GitHub at `https://github.com/nygard/class-dump`.

Keychain Dumper

Another very interesting and useful tool is Keychain Dumper that, as the name suggests, will let you dump the contents from the keychain. Normally, the way an application is granted access to the keychain is specified in its entitlements, which defines the information that can be accessed by that application. The way this tool works is that the binary is signed with a self-signed certificate with wildcard entitlements. Hence, it is able to access all the keychain items. To install `keychain_dumper`, just download the `zip` archive from the GitHub repo `https://github.com/ptoomey3/Keychain-Dumper` and unpack it. Then, you only need to copy the `keychain_dumper` binary to the phone as follows:

```
$ scp keychain_dumper root@usb:/tmp/
```

Then, make sure that `keychain_dumper` is executable and validate that `/private/var/Keychains/keychain-2.db` is world readable. If not, you can set them as follows:

```
# chmod u+x keychain_dumper
# chmod +r /private/var/Keychains/keychain-2.db
```

You should now be able to run the tool without any issues.

```
# ./keychain_dumper
Generic Password
----------------
Service: AirPort
Account: ******** Work
Entitlement Group: apple
Label: (null)
Generic Field: (null)
Keychain Data: s***iami**********
...
...
```

As you can see from the preceding output, by default, `keychain_dumper` only dumps generic and Internet passwords. However, you can also specify optional flags to dump additional information from the keychain, as shown from the help (`-h`) command as follows:

```
# ./keychain_dumper -h
Usage: keychain_dumper [-e]|[-h]|[-agnick]
<no flags>: Dump Password Keychain Items (Generic Password, Internet
Passwords)
-a: Dump All Keychain Items (Generic Passwords, Internet Passwords,
Identities, Certificates, and Keys)
-e: Dump Entitlements
-g: Dump Generic Passwords
-n: Dump Internet Passwords
-i: Dump Identities
-c: Dump Certificates
-k: Dump Keys
```

dumpDecrypted

Executables of an application downloaded from the App Store are encrypted. The dumpDecrypted tool, developed by Stefan Esser (iOS hacker and author of this tool), runs the targeted app and dumps it decrypted from memory to disk. To install dumpDecrypted, download the zip archive from its GitHub page (https://github.com/stefanesser/dumpdecrypted) in your Mac (it is for OSX only), unzip it, and compile the source file by simply typing the make command as follows:

```
$ wget https://github.com/stefanesser/dumpdecrypted/archive/master.zip
$ unzip dumpdecrypted-master.zip
$ cd dumpdecrypted-master
$ make
`xcrun --sdk iphoneos --find gcc` -Os  -Wimplicit -isysroot `xcrun --sdk
iphoneos --show-sdk-path` -F`xcrun --sdk iphoneos --show-sdk-path`/
System/Library/Frameworks -F`xcrun --sdk iphoneos --show-sdk-path`/
System/Library/PrivateFrameworks -arch armv7 -arch armv7s -arch arm64 -c
-o dumpdecrypted.o dumpdecrypted.c

`xcrun --sdk iphoneos --find gcc` -Os  -Wimplicit -isysroot `xcrun --
sdk iphoneos --show-sdk-path` -F`xcrun --sdk iphoneos --show-sdk-
path`/System/Library/Frameworks -F`xcrun --sdk iphoneos --show-sdk-
path`/System/Library/PrivateFrameworks -arch armv7 -arch armv7s -arch
arm64 -dynamiclib -o dumpdecrypted.dylib dumpdecrypted.o
```

Then, simply copy the compiled file into your iPhone:

```
$ scp dumpdecrypted.dylib root@usb:/usr/bin/
```

Application analysis

When analyzing an application, you need to look at all its activities and interactions with the system by analyzing all the traces and artifacts left on the system while running and after it has run, and to/from the system, which means being able to understand how and whom the application communicates with by sending and receiving data. Therefore, you need to look at the three states where data can exist.

Data at rest

With data at rest, we refer to all the data recorded on storage media, in our case, on the mobile device's internal memory. These are the `plist` files, the `sqlite` databases, logs, and any other information we can retrieve directly from the media itself. We will not go much into details here, since this procedure is the same as for the forensic analysis of a specific application that is going through the application directory tree structure to check its files and analyze the system logs. Refer to *Chapter 4, Analyzing iOS Devices,* for more details.

Data in use

Data in use is, as the name suggests, all data being currently used by the application. Such data resides in the memory (RAM) of the device. In a standard malware analysis for computer malwares, memory analysis is, whenever possible, part of the game. Unfortunately for iOS, but in general, for the entire mobile panorama, memory acquisition and analysis is not well developed yet although some utilities/proof-of-concepts to dump the memory have been implemented. However, memory analysis and runtime manipulation/abuse are out of the scope of this book, but you can try yourself and refer to *readmem* (https://github.com/gdbinit/readmem), *memscan* (https://hexplo.it/introducing-memscan/), or a tutorial online (https://blog.netspi.com/ios-tutorial-dumping-the-application-heap-from-memory/) to learn about memory analysis, and *Hacking and Securing iOS Applications, Jonathan Zdziarski, O'Reilly Media,* to learn about runtime manipulation/abuse.

Data in transit

Data in transit refers to any information that is being transferred between two nodes in a network, which is in our case all data sent and received by the target application. Being able to observe and manipulate data sent over the network by an application is extremely interesting and useful for behavioral/dynamic analysis in case of a suspicious app.

Before starting, remember to isolate the device from the networks (all of them), especially if you are analyzing a malicious application. Therefore, create an ad-hoc wireless network that is isolated (not connected to the Internet or to your internal network), then put your iPhone in Airplane Mode and switch on only the Wi-Fi afterwards so that the other network interfaces remain off.

To begin with, you need to route the traffic of the phone through your computer in order to pose yourself as man in the middle. To use the trick in your `ssh` configuration, as we did before, start by launching `iproxy` and establishing an `ssh` connection to your phone as follows:

```
$ iproxy 2222 22
$ ssh usb
```

Then, from your device network configuration, set up an HTTP proxy to manual towards localhost 127.0.0.1 port 8080. It will be redirected to your Mac to port 8080.

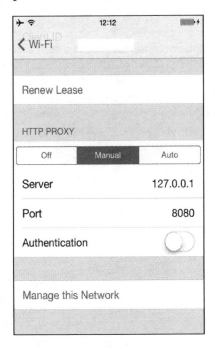

Now that the iPhone is set up, you need to set up a proxy listening on your local host port 8080. **Burp Proxy** is probably the most popular proxy (`http://portswigger.net/burp/`); it is cross-platform and there is a free version that works just fine for our purposes. But there are many others out there, so pick your favorite one. Once an HTTP request has been intercepted, with Burp you can perform several actions such as modifying the request parameters, intercepting and modifying the response, and much more.

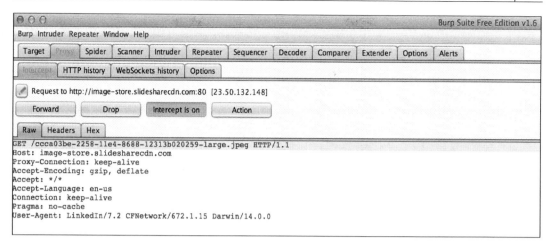

However, although Burp is great at intercepting the HTTP/HTTPS protocol, you may want to have a look at all the traffic, because some applications may not use standard HTTP to communicate, and record it for further analysis on a later stage. To do so, you will need to install **Wireshark**, the standard de facto packet analyzer together with `tcpdump`, and run a capture on your loopback interface 127.0.0.1.

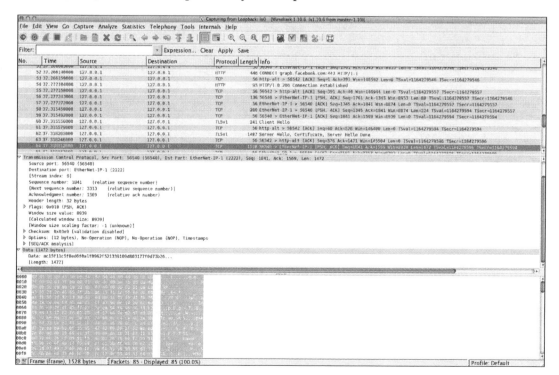

Of course, on a jailbroken iPhone, you have full control and may choose to install and go via `tcpdump` directly on the device.

Automating the analysis

This paragraph will quickly introduce some tools that will help you during the analysis either by speeding up the most common tasks or providing you with some extra and very useful functionalities.

The iOS Reverse Engineering Toolkit

The **iOS Reverse Engineering Toolkit** (`iRET`) is a set of tools that allows you to automate a series of tasks in order to analyze and reverse engineer the iOS applications. The interesting feature of this toolkit is that everything happens directly on the device, while you have a web interface to interact with it. Before installing `iRET`, you will need to install the following dependencies, all of which can be downloaded and installed via Cydia: Python (2.5.1 or 2.7), coreutils, Erica Utilities, file, adv-cmds, Bourne-Again Shell, iOS Toolchain (the CoolStar version), and Darwin CC Tools (coolstar version). The `iRET` application also requires `keychain_dumper` and `dumpDecrypted`, which you should have already installed on your iPhone (see the *Setting up the environment* section). Once all the dependencies and requirements are met, we can finally complete the installation of `iRET`. Download the `zip` archive from the official website, unzip it, and then simply copy the `iRET.deb` file to your iPhone. The link is `https://www.veracode.com/sites/default/files/Resources/Tools/iRETTool.zip`. Then, from your computer, copy `iRET.deb` to the iPhone as follows:

```
$ scp iRET.deb root@usb:/var/root/mytools/
```

Then, from your iPhone, install the package and restart the iPhone:

```
# dpkg -i iRET.deb
```

After restarting the iPhone, you should see the `iRET` application icon on your device. Click on it and it will tell you where to connect your browser to access and manage it:

Then, you just need to insert that address into your browser and you will be prompted with the iRET control panel, where you can perform all the actions available. The following screenshot shows an example of this:

The iRET application helps you in the sense that it automates several tasks that you would always need to run manually in order to analyze an application. Once you select the application to analyze, `iRET` offers different features that can be chosen by selecting one of the different tabs at the top:

- **Binary analysis**: Using `otool`, this option extracts and shows information about the binary. The displayed data includes binary header information; it tells if **Position Independent Executable (PIE)**, Stack Smashing Protection, and **Automatic Resource Counting (ARC)** are enabled, which would reduce the likelihood of finding memory corruption vulnerabilities to attack.

- **Keychain analysis**: This feature automates the execution of the `Keychain_dumper` utility we have installed and seen before.

- **Database analysis**: This feature provides you with a drop-down menu containing all databases (`.db`, `.sqlite`, and `.sqlite3`) found within the selected application. Once a database is selected, it will display the content of the database.

- **Log viewer**: This feature allows you to review the last entries of the system logs, as well as providing you with a drop-down menu with all identified log and text files associated with the selected application.

- **Plist viewer**: This feature allows you to view the content of all of the property list files that were found for the selected application.

- **Header files**: If the binary is encrypted, this feature will automatically decrypt and perform a class dump of the unencrypted binary into separate header files. It will then allow you to display the content of the chosen header.

- **Theos**: This feature allows you to create, edit, save, and build the `theos` tweaks, making use of Cydia Substrate for runtime manipulation.

- **Screenshot**: This feature allows you to view the cached screenshot of the selected application if present.

For more information about Cydia Substrate (also known as MobileSubstrate), Cycript and on how to manipulate the runtime, check out the following links:

- `http://iphonedevwiki.net/index.php/MobileSubstrate`
- `http://www.cycript.org/`

idb

Developed and maintained by Daniel Mayer, `idb` is a tool that simplifies some of the most common tasks related to the iOS application analysis. Originally built with a penetration tester/researcher focus, it can be of great value for any type of application analysis, thanks to the number of tools that incorporates and features offered. Written in Ruby, the installation procedure is quite straightforward; you just need to perform the following commands:

```
$ rvm install 2.1 --enable-shared
$ gem install bundler
$ brew install qt cmake usbmuxd libimobiledevice
$ git clone --recursive https://github.com/dmayer/idb.git
$ cd idb
$ bundle install
$ ruby gidb.rb
```

This is the procedure for Mac OS X. For more information on building and running it on other systems, you can refer to the official page at `https://github.com/dmayer/idb`.

Once you have launched `idb` after following the configuration steps to install some needed tools on the device, you will have to select an application and start the analysis by clicking on **Analyze Binary**. As you can see in the following screenshot, on the left-hand side of the panel, this action will give the first information on the binary itself. As we have seen for `iRET`, it uses `otool` to verify that PIE, Stack Smashing Protection, and ARC are enabled, which would reduce the likelihood of finding memory corruption vulnerabilities to attack. Moreover, if the binary application is encrypted, `idb` will run `dumpdecrypted` to decrypt it before analyzing it. This first action is compulsory in order to enable all the others.

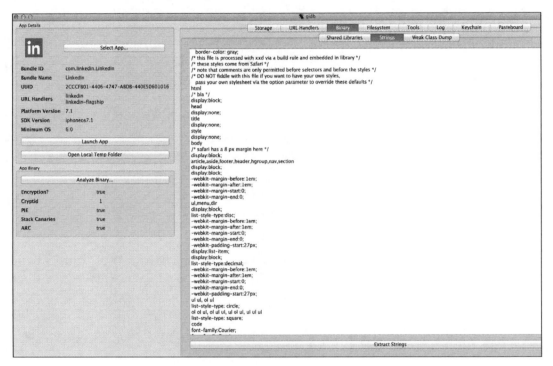

Other information related to the binary app can also be extracted from the **Binary** tab at the top of the right-hand side panel. Still from the preceding screenshot, you can see idb extracting all the strings from the decrypted binary. This is a standard step you would do when analyzing standard computer malware. This is of great use since here you may find the API keys, credentials, encryption keys, URLs, and other useful hints. From a static analysis perspective, idb binary analysis allows you to dump all the class information.

Talking about data at rest, under the **Storage** tab, you will be able to analyze all the files related to your target application, such as plist, the sqlite databases, and Cache.db, which contains cached HTTP requests/responses and offline data cached by web applications such as images, HTML, JavaScript, style sheets, and more. The idb tool will also allow you to navigate through the app tree structure from the **Filesystem** tab, taking and storing subsequent different snapshots to navigate and compare at a later stage.

Two other interesting functionalities provided are the **URL Handlers**, which shows you the list of the URL handlers and includes a basic fuzzer that can be used to fuzz input data via the URL schemes, and the **Keychain** dumper, which is a functionality that allows you to dump the keychain similar to iRET but using keychain_dump from iphone_dataprotection Sogeti's tool (https://code.google.com/p/iphone-dataprotection/).

The **Tools** tab contains several different tools that are quite handy; they are as follows:

- **Background screenshot**: Although this tool is more useful for forensics/security purposes, it looks for an eventual screenshot taken by the system when putting the application in the background by pushing the Home button.

- **Certification manager**: This tool will speed up the management and installation of the CA certificate. This is extremely useful, for example, when using Burp for HTTPS traffic and an application that actually checks that SSL is in place.

- **/etc/hosts file editor**: As we have seen before for the data in transit, apps not always use the HTTP/s protocol, so Burp will not intercept. With this editor, you can quickly access and modify /etc/hosts of the iPhone in order to redirect the traffic towards custom services you may have fired up for the analysis.

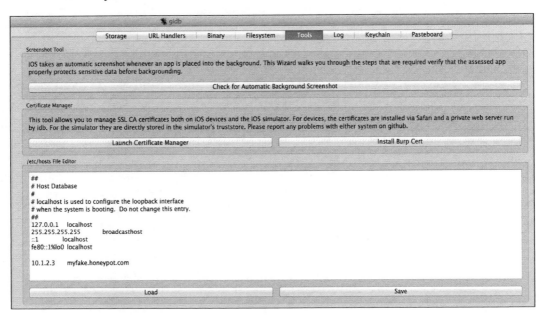

Last but not least, idb offers a real-time log (syslog) and pasteboard viewer (refer to the following screenshot) via the **Log** and **Pasteboard** tabs, respectively. Although it may not seem of great use to monitor the pasteboard when you are the one testing the application, it may surprise you to know that applications use the pasteboard also for **Inter-Process Communication (IPC)**. By default, idb monitors only the main (default) pasteboard, but you can add additional pasteboard names to the list on the right-hand side so that you will also be able to monitor the private pasteboards.

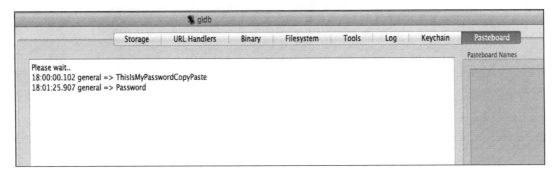

Regarding the **Log** panel, `idb` includes both system messages and any log statements that the app produces using `NSLog`, which often discloses sensitive data.

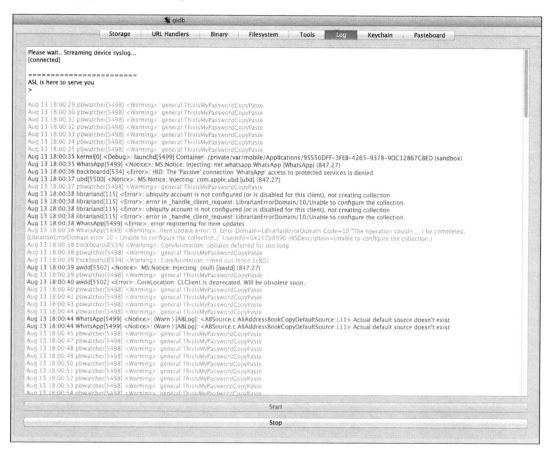

Summary

In this chapter, we introduced some tools for the analyzing of the iOS applications, suspicious or not, mainly from a behavioral/dynamic point of view. You learned how to quickly analyze the binary, how to review the data and logs produced by the targeted application, how to intercept, manipulate, and analyze the data sent and received over the network, and how to automate most of the tasks with ad-hoc toolkits, such as `iRET` and `idb`.

Self-test questions

1. Which tool can be used to extract Objective-C class information from iOS applications?

    1. OpenSSH
    2. MobileTerminal
    3. class-dump-z
    4. Keychain Dumper

2. Which tool can be used to dump an unencrypted application from memory?

    1. usbmuxd
    2. Keychain Dumper
    3. dumpDecrypted
    4. OpenSSH

3. Which tool can be used to verify the pasteboard content?

    1. dumpDecrypted
    2. iRet
    3. iLoot
    4. idb

4. Which tools would you use to best analyze data in transit?

    1. Burp Proxy + Wireshark
    2. iproxy + Wireshark
    3. dumpDecrypted + tcpdump
    4. iRET + iproxy

5. Which set of tools allow automating a series of tasks in order to analyze and reverse engineer iOS Applications?

    1. iLoot
    2. iRet
    3. class-dump-z
    4. dumpDecrypted

References

Publications freely available

Here's list of publications that are available for free:

- *Guidelines on Mobile Device Forensics, Rick Ayers, Sam Brothers, Wayne Jansen, NIST Special Publication 800-101, 2014* is available at `http://nvlpubs.nist.gov/nistpubs/SpecialPublications/NIST.SP.800-101r1.pdf`

- *Guidelines for Managing the Security of Mobile Devices in the Enterprise, Murugiah Souppaya, Karen Scarafone, NIST Special Publication 800-124, 2013* is available at `http://nvlpubs.nist.gov/nistpubs/SpecialPublications/NIST.SP.800-124r1.pdf`

- *Technical Considerations for Vetting 3rd Party Mobile Applications (Draft), Jeffrey Voas, Steve Quirolgico, Christoph Michael, Karen Scarafone, NIST Special Publication 800-163 (Draft), 2014* is available at `http://csrc.nist.gov/publications/drafts/800-163/sp800_163_draft.pdf`

- *iOS Forensic, Christian Javier D'Orazio, 2013* is available at `https://wiki.cis.unisa.edu.au/wki/images/7/7c/DORAZIO_iOS_Forensics_Final_Revise.pdf`

- *iOS Forensics Investigative Methods, Jonathan Zdziarski, 2012* is available at `http://www.zdziarski.com/blog/wp-content/uploads/2013/05/iOS-Forensic-Investigative-Methods.pdf`

- *Extracting SQLite Records, Ivo Pooters, Pascal Arends, Steffen Moorrees, 2011* is available at `http://sandbox.dfrws.org/2011/fox-it/DFRWS2011_results/Report/Sqlite_carving_extractAndroidData.pdf`

- *SIM and USIM Filesystem: A Forensics Perspective, Antonio Savoldi, Paolo Gubian, Proceedings of the 2007 ACM Symposium on Applied Computing, 2007* is available at `http://www.researchgate.net/publication/220998796_SIM_and_USIM_filesystem_a_forensics_perspective/links/0912f510991d40f98b000000`

- *A Hypothesis-based Approach to Digital Forensic Investigations, Brian Carrier, CERIAS Tech Report 2006-06* is available at `https://www.cerias.purdue.edu/assets/pdf/bibtex_archive/2006-06.pdf`

- *A Road Map for Digital Forensic Research, 2001* is a report from the first **Digital Forensic Research Workshop (DFRWS)**, which is available at `http://www.dfrws.org/2001/dfrws-rm-final.pdf`

- *Forensic analysis of social networking applications on mobile devices, Noora Al Mutawa, Ibrahim Baggili, Andrew Marrington, Elsevier Ltd.* is available at `http://www.dfrws.org/2012/proceedings/DFRWS2012-3.pdf`

Tools, manuals, and reports

Here is a list of some online tools, manuals, and reports:

- *Elcomsoft iOS Forensic Toolkit Guide, Colby Lahaie, Champlain College* is available at `http://www.champlain.edu/Documents/LCDI/Elcomsoft_iOS_Forensic_Toolkit_Guide.pdf`

- *Cellebrite iOS Device Physical Extraction Manual, Cellebrite* is available at `http://www.ume-update.com/UFED/iOS_User_Manual.pdf`

- *What Happens When You Press that Button?, Cellebrite* is available at `https://www.cellebrite.com/collateral/Explaining_Cellebrite_UFED_Data_Extraction_Processes.pdf`

- *Lantern Version 2.0.4 Evaluation Report, NIJ Electronic Crime Technology Center of Excellence* is available at `https://www.justnet.org/pdf/12-21-11%20lantern%20report.pdf`

- *Test Results for Mobile Device Acquisition Tool: Lantern v2.3, NIST* is available at `https://ncjrs.gov/pdffiles1/nij/241154.pdf`

- *iOS Forensics with Open-Source Tools, Andrey Belenko, Zeronights, 2014* is available at `http://2014.zeronights.org/assets/files/slides/belenko.pdf`

Apple's official documentation

Official Apple documentation can be downloaded directly from its website. The most interesting papers about security and forensics are:

- *Legal Process Guidelines, U.S. Law Enforcement* is available at `https://www.apple.com/legal/more-resources/law-enforcement/`

- *iOS Security, October 2014* is available at `https://www.apple.com/privacy/docs/iOS_Security_Guide_Oct_2014.pdf`

- *iPhone User Guide* is available at `http://help.apple.com/iphone/` and `http://manuals.info.apple.com/MANUALS/1000/MA1565/en_US/iphone_user_guide.pdf`

- iPhone Tech Specs is available at `http://support.apple.com/specs/#iphone`

- *iPad User Guide* is available at `http://support.apple.com/manuals/#ipad` and `http://manuals.info.apple.com/MANUALS/1000/MA1595/en_US/ipad_user_guide.pdf`

- iPad Tech Specs is available at `http://support.apple.com/specs/#ipad`

- *iPod touch User Guide* is available at `http://support.apple.com/manuals/#ipodtouch` and `http://manuals.info.apple.com/MANUALS/1000/MA1596/en_US/ipod_touch_user_guide.pdf`

- iPod Touch Tech Specs is available at `http://support.apple.com/specs/#ipodtouch`

- How to find the serial number, IMEI, MEID, CDN, and ICCID number for iOS can be viewed at `http://support.apple.com/kb/ht4061`

- Back up and restore your iOS device with iCloud or iTunes can be viewed at `http://support.apple.com/kb/HT1766`

- Information about iOS backups (iTunes) is available at `http://support.apple.com/kb/ht4946`

- Protect your iOS device using the information available at `http://support.apple.com/kb/HT5874`

- Forgot passcode or device disabled (iOS) information is available at `http://support.apple.com/kb/HT1212`

- iCloud storage and backup overview is available at `http://support.apple.com/kb/PH12519`

- Information about troubleshooting and creating an iCloud backup is available at `http://support.apple.com/kb/TS3992`

- HFS Plus Volume Format is available at `https://developer.apple.com/legacy/library/technotes/tn/tn1150.html`

Device security and data protection

If the reader is interested in learning more about the security of iOS devices, the following are the most interesting researches carried out:

- *Identifying Back Doors, Attack Points, and Surveillance Mechanisms in iOS Devices, Jonathan Zdziarski, Digital Investigation, Volume 11, Issue 1, March 2014,* is available at http://www.sciencedirect.com/science/article/pii/ S1742287614000036. A related presentation is available at http://www. zdziarski.com/blog/wp-content/uploads/2014/07/iOS_Backdoors_ Attack_Points_Surveillance_Mechanisms.pdf.

- *iPhone security model & vulnerabilities, Cedric Halbronn, Jean Sigwald, Sogeti Lab, 2010* is available at http://esec-lab.sogeti.com/dotclear/public/ publications/10-hitbkl-iphone.pdf.

- *iPhone data protection in depth, Jean-Baptiste Bédrune, Jean Sigwald, Sogeti Lab, 2012* is available at http://blog.pollito.fr/public/2012/06/11- hitbamsterdam-iphonedataprotection.pdf.

- *Forensics iOS, Jean-Baptiste Bédrune, Jean Sigwald* is available at https://www. sstic.org/media/SSTIC2012/SSTIC-actes/forensicsios/SSTIC2012- Slides-forensicsios-sigwald_bedrune.pdf.

- *Overcoming data protection to re-enable iOS forensics, Andrey Belenko, Black Hat USA, 2011* is available at https://media.blackhat.com/bh-us-11/ Belenko/BH_US_11_Belenko_iOS_Forensics_Slides.pdf.

- *Handling iOS encryption in a forensic investigation, Jochem van Kerkwijk, Universiteit van Amsterdam, 2011* is available at http://www.delaat.net/ rp/2010-2011/p26/report.pdf.

- *iOS Keychain Weakness FAQ, Jens Heider, Rachid El Khayari, Fraunhofer Institute for Secure Information Technology (SIT), 2012* is available at http://sit.sit. fraunhofer.de/studies/en/sc-iphone-passwords-faq.pdf.

- *Lost iPhone? Lost Passwords!, Jens Heider, Matthias Boll, Fraunhofer Institute for Secure Information Technology (SIT), 2011* is available at https://www. sit.fraunhofer.de/fileadmin/dokumente/studien_und_technical_ reports/Whitepaper_Lost_iPhone.pdf.

- *iOS Encryption Systems, Peter Teufl, Thomas Zefferer, Christof Stromberger, Christoph Heckhenblaikner, Institute for Applied Information Processing and Communications, 2014* is available at http://www.a-sit.at/pdfs/ Technologiebeobachtung/ios-encryption-systems.pdf.

Device hardening

Information on how to harden an iOS device can be found in the following papers:

- *CIS Apple iOS 8 Benchmark, Center for Internet Security, 2014* is available at `http://benchmarks.cisecurity.org/downloads/show-single/?file=appleios8.100`

- *CIS Apple iOS 7 Benchmark, Center for Internet Security, 2013* is available at `http://benchmarks.cisecurity.org/downloads/show-single/?file=appleios7.100`

- *iOS Hardening Configuration Guide, Australian Government – Department of Defence, 2012* is available at `http://www.asd.gov.au/publications/iOS5_Hardening_Guide.pdf`

- *Security Configuration Recommendations for Apple iOS 5 Devices, National Security Agency, 2012* is available at `http://www.nsa.gov/ia/_files/os/applemac/apple_ios_5_guide.pdf`

iTunes backup

Among the papers and articles related to the iTunes backup structure and analysis the most interesting are:

- Information about MBDB and MBDX formats can be found at `http://code.google.com/p/iphonebackupbrowser/wiki/MbdbMbdxFormat`

- *iPhone 3GS Forensics: Logical analysis using Apple iTunes Backup Utility, Mona Bader, Ibrahim Baggili, Small Scale Digital Device Forensics Journal, 2010* is available at `http://securitylearn.net/wp-content/uploads/iOS%20Resources/iPhone%203GS%20Forensics%20Logical%20analysis%20using%20Apple%20iTunes%20Backup%20Utility.pdf`

- *Forensic Analysis of iPhone backups* is available at `http://www.exploit-db.com/wp-content/themes/exploit/docs/19767.pdf`

- Information about Encrypted iTunes backups by Hal Pomeranz in the video *Forensic Lunch, 2014* is available at `http://www.youtube.com/watch?v=mNLOokxME5A`

- Information about iTunes backup analysis by *Vladimir Katalov, 2013, Elcomsoft Blog* can be found at `http://blog.crackpassword.com/2013/09/itunes_backup_analysis/`

- *Advanced Smartphone Forensics, Vladimir Katalov, ElcomSoft Co. Ltd, 2014* is available at `http://elcomsoft.com/presentations/nullcon2014.pdf`

- *Using PC Backups in Mobile Forensics, Gilad Sahar, Cellebrite* is available at `http://thetrainingco.com/Techno-2013-PDF/TUESDAY/T1%20Sahar%20-%20Using%20PC%20Backups%20in%20Mobile%20Forensics.pdf`

- *Looking to iPhone backup files for evidence extraction, Clinton Carpene, School of Computer and Security Science, Edith Cowan University* is available at `http://igneous.scis.ecu.edu.au/proceedings/2011/adf/carpene.pdf`

- *iPhone Backup Files. A penetration Tester's Treasure, Darren Manners, The SANS Institute, 2011* is available at `http://www.sans.org/reading-room/whitepapers/testing/iphone-backup-files-penetration-testers-treasure-33859`

iCloud Backup

Various presentations about iCloud Backup illustrate the most interesting concepts from a security and forensics point of view:

- *Advanced Smartphone Forensics, Vladimir Katalov, ElcomSoft Co. Ltd, 2014* is available at `http://elcomsoft.com/presentations/nullcon2014.pdf`

- *iCloud Keychain and iOS 7 Data Protection, Andrey Belenko, ViaForensics, 2013* is available at `https://speakerdeck.com/belenko/icloud-keychain-and-ios-7-data-protection`

- *Modern Smartphone Forensics, Vladimir Katalov, HITBSecConf, 2013* is available at `http://conference.hitb.org/hitbsecconf2013kul/materials/D2T2%20-%20Vladimir%20Katalov%20-%20Cracking%20and%20Analyzing%20Apple's%20iCloud%20Protocol.pdf`

- *Apple iCloud Inside out, Vladimir Katalov, HITBSecConf, 2013* is available at `https://deepsec.net/docs/Slides/2013/DeepSec_2013_Vladimir_Katalov_-_Cracking_And_Analyzing_Apple_iCloud_Protocols.pdf`

- *Cracking and Analyzing Apple iCloud backups, Find My iPhone, Document Storage, Oleg Afonin, REcon, 2013* is available at `https://www.elcomsoft.com/PR/recon_2013.pdf`

Application data analysis

Dedicated articles, presentations and papers on specific applications data analysis are provided in the following list:

- *iOS Application Forensics* is available at `http://www.scribd.com/doc/57611934/CEIC-2011-iOS-Application-Forensics`

- *Third Party Application Forensics on Apple Mobile Devices, Alex Levinson, Bill Stackpole, Daryl Johnson* is available at `http://www.researchgate.net/publication/224221519_Third_Party_Application_Forensics_on_Apple_Mobile_Devices`

- The *Investigation iOS Phone Images, File Dumps & Backups* article is available at `http://www.magnetforensics.com/investigating-ios-phone-images-file-dumps-backups/`

- The *Analysis Of iOS Notes App* article is available at `http://articles.forensicfocus.com/2013/11/02/analysis-of-ios-notes-app/`

- *Forensic Artifacts of the ChatOn Instant Messaging application, Iqbal A., Marrington A., Baggili I., IEEE* is available at `http://ieeexplore.ieee.org/xpl/articleDetails.jsp?reload=true&arnumber=6911538`

- *Forensic analysis of social networking applications on mobile devices, Noora Al Mutawa, Ibrahim Baggili, Andrew Marrington, Elsevier Ltd.* is available at `http://www.dfrws.org/2012/proceedings/DFRWS2012-3.pdf`

- The *From iPhone to Access Point* article is available at `http://articles.forensicfocus.com/2013/09/03/from-iphone-to-access-point/`

- *Analysis of WeChat on iPhone, Feng Gao, Ying Zhang, Atlantis Press* can be downloaded from `http://www.atlantis-press.com/php/download_paper.php?id=10185`

- *Know Your Suspect - Uncovering Hidden Evidence from Mobile Devices with Oxygen Forensics* is available at `http://www.forensicfocus.com/c/aid=74/webinars/2014/know-your-suspect---uncovering-hidden-evidence-from-mobile-devices-with-oxygen-forensics/`

- Information about iPhone Call History Database is available at `http://avi.alkalay.net/2011/12/iphone-call-history.html`

- *iPhone Call History, Detective Richard Gilleland* is available at `http://cryptome.org/isp-spy/iphone-spy2.pdf`

- The *Who's Texting? The iOS6 sms.db* article is available at `http://linuxsleuthing.blogspot.it/2013/05/ios6-photo-streams-recover-deleted.html`

- The *Parsing the iPhone SMS Database* article is available at `http://linuxsleuthing.blogspot.it/2011/02/parsing-iphone-sms-database.html`

- The *Addressing the iOS 6 Address Book and SQLite Pitfalls* article is available at `http://linuxsleuthing.blogspot.it/2012/10/addressing-ios6-address-book-and-sqlite.html`

- The *iOS 6 Photo Streams: "Recover" Deleted Camera Roll Photos* article is available at `http://linuxsleuthing.blogspot.it/2013/05/ios6-photo-streams-recover-deleted.html`

- The *Recovering Data from Deleted SQLite Records: Redux* article is available at `http://linuxsleuthing.blogspot.it/2013/09/recovering-data-from-deleted-sqlite.html`

- The *SQLite Data Parser to Recover Deleted Records* blog is available at `http://az4n6.blogspot.it/2014/09/sqlite-deleted-data-parser-gui-added.html`

- *Social Networking Applications on Mobile Devices, Noora Al Mutawa, Ibrahim Baggili, Andrew Marrington* is available at `http://www.ccse.kfupm.edu.sa/~ahmadsm/coe589-121/almutawa2012-social-network-mobile-slides.pdf`

- *Forensic Acquisition and Analysis of Tango VoIP, Nhien-An Le-Khac, Christos Sgaras, M-Tahar Kechadi* is available at `https://www.insight-centre.org/sites/default/files/publications/icciet-2014.pdf`

- *Challenges in Obtaining and Analyzing Information from Mobile Devices, Davydov, 2014* is available at `http://computerforensicsblog.champlain.edu/wp-content/uploads/2014/05/Challenges-in-Obtaining-and-Analyzing-Information-from-Mobile-Devices-DavydovO-5-20-2014.pdf`

- The Smartphone Forensics poster by SANS DFIR is available at `https://digital-forensics.sans.org/media/DFIR-Smartphone-Forensics-Poster.pdf`

Related books

Other previous books on the same topic are:

- Bommisetty, Satish, Tamma, Rohit, Mahalik Heather, *Practical Mobile Forensics*, Packt Publishing, 2014

- Zdziarski, Jonathan, *Hacking and Securing iOS Applications*, O'Reilly, 2012

- Miller, Charlie, Blazakis, Dyonysus, Dai Zovi, Dino, Esser, Stefan, Iozzo, Vincenzo, Weinmann, Ralf-Philip, *iOS Hacker's Handbook*, John Wiley & Sons, 2012

- Hogg, Andrew, Strzempka, Katie, *iPhone and iOS Forensics: Investigation, Analysis and Mobile Security for Apple iPhone, iPad and iOS Devices*, Syngress, 2011

- Casey, Eoghan, *Digital Evidence and Computer Crime: Forensic Science, Computers, and the Internet Third Edition*, Academic Press, 2011

- Morrissey, Sean, *iOS Forensic Analysis: for iPhone, iPad, and iPod touch*, Apress, 2010

- Jonathan, Zdziarski, *iPhone Forensics*, O'Reilly, 2008

- Kubasiak, Ryan, Morrissey, Sean, *Mac OS X, iPod, and iPhone Forensics Analysis Toolkit*, Syngress, 2008

- Casey, Eoghan, *Digital Evidence and Computer Crime First Edition*, Academic Press, 2000

B
Tools for iOS Forensics

Acquisition tools

The list of physical acquisition tools (iPhone 2G/3G/3GS/4, iPad 1, iPod touch 1/2/3/4) is as follows:

- **UFED Physical Analyzer**: http://www.cellebrite.com
- **Elcomsoft iOS Forensic Toolkit**: http://www.elcomsoft.com/
- **AccessData Mobile Phone Examiner Plus**: http://www.accessdata.com/solutions/digital-forensics/mobile-phone-examiner
- **Lantern**: https://katanaforensics.com/
- **XRY**: http://www.msab.com/
- **iXAM forensics**: http://www.ixam-forensics.com/
- **iPhone data protection tools**: https://code.google.com/p/iphone-dataprotection/
- **Zdziarski Method**: http://www.iosresearch.org/
- **Paraben's Device Seizure**: https://www.paraben.com/device-seizure.html

For physical acquisition tools (jailbroken iPhone 4s/5/5c, iPad 2/3/4, iPad Mini 1) you can use Elcomsoft iOS Forensic Toolkit.

For advanced logical acquisition tools (all models) you can choose UFED Physical Analyzer.

A list of logical/backup acquisition tools (all models) is as follows:

- **iTunes**: https://www.apple.com/itunes/download/
- **Libimobiledevice**: http://www.libimobiledevice.org/
- **UFED Physical Analyzer/UFED 4PC/Ufed Touch**: http://www.cellebrite.com
- **Oxygen Forensic® Suite Standard/Analyst**: http://www.oxygen-forensic.com/en/
- **Mobiledit Forensic**: http://www.mobiledit.com/forensic
- **AccessData Mobile Phone Examiner Plus**: http://www.accessdata.com/solutions/digital-forensics/mobile-phone-examiner
- **Lantern**: https://katanaforensics.com/
- **XRY**: http://www.msab.com/
- **Paraben's Device Seizure**: https://www.paraben.com/device-seizure.html

iDevice browsing tools and other nonforensic tools

A list of iDevice browsing tools and other nonforensic tools is as follows:

- **Wondershare Dr.Fone iOS**: http://www.wondershare.com/data-recovery-mac/mac-iphone-data-recovery.html
- **iSkysoft iPhone Data Recovery**: http://www.iskysoft.com/iphone-data-recovery/
- **iFunBox**: http://www.i-funbox.com/
- **iMazing**: http://imazing.com/
- **iExplorer**: http://www.macroplant.com/iexplorer/
- **PhoneView**: http://www.ecamm.com/mac/phoneview/

iDevice backup analyzer

A list of iDevice backup analyzers is as follows:

- **UFED Physical Analyzer/UFED 4PC/Ufed Touch**: http://www.cellebrite.com

- **Oxygen Forensic® Suite Standard/Analyst**: `http://www.oxygen-forensic.com/en/`

- **Elcomsoft Phone Viewer**: `http://www.elcomsoft.com/epv.html`

- **Mobiledit Forensic**: `http://www.mobiledit.com/forensic`

- **AccessData Mobile Phone Examiner Plus**: `http://www.accessdata.com/solutions/digital-forensics/mobile-phone-examiner`

- **iPhone Backup Analyzer**: `http://www.ipbackupanalyzer.com/`

- **iPhone Analyzer**: `http://www.crypticbit.com/zen/products/iphoneanalyzer`

- **iPhone Backup Browser**: `https://code.google.com/p/iphonebackupbrowser/`

- **Super Crazy Awesome iPhone Backup Extractor**: `http://supercrazyawesome.com/`

- **Apple iTunes Backup Parser EnScript**: `http://www.proactivediscovery.com/apple-itunes-backup-parser/`

- **iBackupBot**: `http://www.icopybot.com/itunes-backup-manager.htm`

- **iPhone Backup Extractor**: `http://www.iphonebackupextractor.com/`

- **iPhone Backup Viewer**: `http://www.imactools.com/iphonebackupviewer/`

- **iBackup Extractor**: `http://www.wideanglesoftware.com/ibackupextractor/`

- **Smsiphone.org**: `http://www.smsiphone.org/`

- **iTunes Backup Extractor**: `http://www.backuptrans.com/itunes-backup-extractor.html`

iDevice encrypted backup

A list of tools to analyze an iDevice encrypted backup is as follows:

- **Elcomsoft Phone Password Breaker**: `http://www.elcomsoft.com/eppb.html`

- **iPhone Backup Unlocker**: `http://www.windowspasswordsrecovery.com/product/iphone-backup-unlocker.htm`

- **Mbdb file parser**: `https://github.com/halpomeranz/mbdbls`

iCloud Backup

A list of tools to analyze an iCloud Backup is as follows:

- **Elcomsoft Phone Password Breaker**: http://www.elcomsoft.com/eppb.html
- **Wondershare Dr.Fone iOS**: http://www.wondershare.com/data-recovery-mac/mac-iphone-data-recovery.html
- **iPhone Data Recovery**: http://www.tenorshare.com/products/iphone-data-recovery-win.html
- iLoot: https://github.com/hackappcom/iloot

Jailbreaking tools

For more information on the jailbreaking tools, refer to the iPhone Wiki jailbreaking tools page at http://theiphonewiki.com/wiki/Jailbreak.

iOS 8

For iOS 8, refer to the following list:

- **Pangu**: http://en.pangu.io/
- **Taig**: http://www.taig.com/en/

iOS 7

For iOS 7, refer to the following list:

- **Pangu**: http://en.7.pangu.io/
- **Evasi0n7**: http://evasi0n.com/
- **Geeksn0w**: http://geeksn0w.it/

iOS 6

For iOS 6, refer to the following list:

- **Evasi0n**: http://evasi0n.com/iOS6/
- **Redsn0w**: http://blog.iphone-dev.org/tagged/redsn0w
- **Sn0wbreeze**: http://ih8sn0w.com/
- **P0sixspwn**: http://p0sixspwn.com/

Data analysis

All the acquisition tools previously illustrated also have analysis features; for this reason here we list the tools only dedicated to data analysis/parsing.

Forensic toolkit

A list of forensic toolkits is as follows:

- **AccessData FTK**: http://accessdata.com/solutions/digital-forensics/forensic-toolkit-ftk
- **GuidanceSoftware Encase Forensic**: https://www.guidancesoftware.com/products/Pages/encase-forensic/overview.aspx
- **X-Ways Forensics**: http://www.x-ways.net/forensics/index-m.html
- **WinHex**: http://www.x-ways.net/winhex/
- **BlackBag Blacklight**: https://www.blackbagtech.com/software-products/blacklight-6/blacklight.html

SQLite viewer

The tools to analyse SQLite databases are as follows:

- **SQLite Database Browser**: http://sqlitebrowser.org/
- **SQLite Expert**: http://www.sqliteexpert.com/
- **SQLite Studio**: http://sqlitestudio.pl/
- **SQLite Manager**: https://addons.mozilla.org/en-US/firefox/addon/sqlite-manager/
- **SQLite Spy**: http://www.yunqa.de/delphi/doku.php/products/sqlitespy/index
- **SQLite Forensic Reporter**: http://www.filesig.co.uk/sqlite-forensic-reporter.html

SQLite record carver

The tools for SQLite record carver are as follows:

- **SQLite Recovery Python Parser**: http://az4n6.blogspot.it/2013/11/python-parser-to-recover-deleted-sqlite.html and https://github.com/mdegrazia/SQLite-Deleted-Records-Parser

- **Epilog**: http://www.cclgroupltd.com/product/epilog-sqlite-forensic-tool/
- **Oxygen Forensics SQLite Viewer**: http://www.oxygen-forensic.com/en/features/analyst/data-viewers/sqlite-viewer
- **SQLite Recovery**: http://sandersonforensics.com/forum/content.php?190-SQLite-Recovery
- **Undark**: http://pldaniels.com/undark/

Plist viewer

The tools to analyse Plist files are as follows:

- **Plist Editor Pro for Windows**: http://www.icopybot.com/plist-editor.htm
- **Oxygen Forensics Plist Viewer**: http://www.oxygen-forensic.com/en/features/analyst/data-viewers/plist-viewer
- **PlistEdit Pro**: http://fatcatsoftware.com/plisteditpro/
- **Pip**: http://www.cclgroupltd.com/product/pip-xml-and-plist-parser/

iOS analysis suite

The most interesting iOS analysis suites are as follows:

- **Internet Evidence Finder**: http://www.magnetforensics.com/
- **BlackLight**: https://www.blackbagtech.com/
- **iPhone Tools**: https://code.google.com/p/linuxsleuthing/downloads/list

App analysis tools

The app analysis tools are listed as follows:

- **SkypeExtractor**: http://www.skypextractor.com/
- **SkypeLogView**: http://nirsoft.net/utils/skype_log_view.html
- **Safari Forensic Tools**: http://jafat.sourceforge.net/files.html
- **iPhone History Parser**: http://az4n6.blogspot.it/2014/07/safari-and-iphone-internet-history.html
- **iThmb Converter**: http://www.ithmbconverter.com/

- **Ultra File Opener**: http://www.ultrafileopener.com/formats/ithmb/
- **class-dump-z**: https://code.google.com/p/networkpx/wiki/class_dump_z
- **Keychain Dumper**: https://github.com/ptoomey3/Keychain-Dumper

Consolidated.db

The tools for Consolidated.db are as follows:

- **iStalkr**: http://www.evigator.com/free-apps/
- **iPhone Tracker**: http://petewarden.github.io/iPhoneTracker/
- **iOS Tracker**: http://tom.zickel.org/iostracker/

App reverse engineering tools

The app reverse engineering tools are as follows:

- **class-dump-z**: https://code.google.com/p/networkpx/wiki/class_dump_z
- **Keychain Dumper**: https://github.com/ptoomey3/Keychain-Dumper
- **Dump Decrypted**: https://github.com/stefanesser/dumpdecrypted
- **Read Mem**: https://github.com/gdbinit/readmem
- **iOS Reverse Engineering Toolkit (iRET)**: https://www.veracode.com/iret-ios-reverse-engineering-toolkit
- **Idb**: https://github.com/dmayer/idb

C
Self-test Answers

Chapter 1: Digital and Mobile Forensics

Question No.	Correct option
1	3
2	4
3	2
4	3

Chapter 2: Introduction to iOS Devices

Question No.	Correct option
1	3
2	2
3	4
4	3
5	4
6	3

Chapter 3: Evidence Acquisition from iDevices

Question No.	Correct option
1	3
2	1
3	1
4	2
5	2

Chapter 4: Analyzing iOS Devices

Question No.	Correct option
1	1
2	4
3	3
4	3
5	2
6	2
7	3
8	3

Chapter 5: Evidence Acquisition and Analysis from iTunes Backup

Question No.	Correct option
1	1
2	2
3	4
4	2

Chapter 6: Evidence Acquisition and Analysis from iCloud

Question No.	Correct option
1	3
2	2
3	4
4	3

Chapter 7: Applications and Malware Analysis

Question No.	Correct option
1	3
2	3
3	4
4	1
5	2

Index

A

Access Control List (ACL) **35**
AccessData FTK
  URL **185**
AccessData Mobile Phone Examiner Plus
  URL **181**
acquisition
  about **17**
  file system **16**
  logical **16**
  physical **16**
  to reporting **16**
address book **91**
advanced logical acquisition
  with UFED Physical Analyzer **66-68**
alternate volume header **36**
analysis, automating
  about **162**
  idb **165-169**
  iOS Reverse Engineering
    Toolkit (iRET) **162-165**
app analysis tools **186**
Apple
  documentation, URL **173**
  law enforcement support **78, 79**
  operating system versions, URL **32**
Apple iTunes Backup Parser EnScript
  URL **183**
application, analysis
  about **158**
  data, at rest **159**
  data, in transit **159-162**
  data, in use **159**
application data analysis
  URL **176**

Application Processor
  URL **30**
app reverse engineering tools **187**
audio recordings **91**
authentication token
  extracting, from iCloud Control Panel **145**

B

backup acquisition. *See* logical acquisition
BigBoss recommended tools **154**
BlackBag Blacklight
  URL **185, 186**
Bluetooth
  URL **24**
boot process, iOS **49**
Burp Proxy
  URL **160**

C

calendar **92**
call history **93, 94**
chain of custody **14, 15**
CIS Apple iOS 7 Benchmark
  URL **175**
CIS Apple iOS 8 Benchmark
  URL **175**
class-dump-z command
  about **156**
  URL **155**
clipboard **99**
cloud storage applications
  Dropbox iOS app **108**
  Google Drive iOS app **109, 110**
clumps **36**
collision **18**

Consolidated.db tools 187
Consolidated GPS cache 100
cross-searching data
  Aggregated Contacts 116
  Dictionaries 116
  Links and Stats 116
  Social Graph 116
  Timeline 116
Cycript
  URL 165
Cydia Substrate (MobileSubstrate) 165

D

data
  storing, ways 85-88
data analysis/parsing 185
databases 89
data partition 42, 43
data protection
  about 111
  URL 174
data recovery
  deleted 111
data storing, ways
  databases 89
  property list files 89
  timestamps 88
Dedicated File (DF) 19
DEFT 8.1
  URL 33
device hardening
  URL 175
device partition 41
device security
  URL 174
digital evidence 9, 10
Digital Forensic Research Workshop
      (DFRWS)
  about 8
  URL 172
digital forensics 7, 8
direct acquisition 58
Dkey (Class D Key) 50
Dropbox iOS app 108
dumpDecrypted tool
  about 158

URL 158

E

Elcomsoft iOS Forensic Toolkit
  physical acquisition with 76-78
  URL 181
Elcomsoft Phone Password
      Breaker (EPPB)
  about 141
  and iDevice backup acquisition, with
      authentication token 145-147
  and iDevice backup acquisition, with
      username and password 141-144
  iTunes encrypted backup
      cracking with 131-135
  URL 145, 183
Elcomsoft Phone Viewer
  URL 183
Electronic Chip ID (ECID)
  about 52
  URL 52
e-mail 94, 95
EMF 50, 111
environment
  class-dump-z command 155, 156
  dumpDecrypted 158
  Keychain Dumper 156, 157
  setting up 153
Epilog
  URL 186
Evasi0n
  URL 75
Evasi0n7
  URL 184
evidence
  collecting 11-13
  identifying 11-13
  integrity 17, 18
  preserving 11-13
extraction flowchart 80, 81

F

Facebook 107, 108
Find My Phone feature 189
forensic toolkit 185

forensic tools
logical acquisition with 60
physical acquisition with 69, 70

G

Geeksn0w
URL 184
Google Drive iOS app 109, 110
GuidanceSoftware Encase Forensic
URL 185

H

hash value 17
HFS+ file system
about 35-40
Allocation File 35
Attributes File 35
Catalog File 35
Extents Overflow File 35
Startup File 35
Volume Header File 35

I

iBackupBot
URL 183
iBackup Extractor
URL 183
iBoot 49
iCloud
iDevice backup 140, 141
iCloud Backup 184
iCloud Control Panel
about 140
URL 145
iCloud Control Panel, artifacts
AccountDSID 149
AccountID 149
DisplayName 149
IsPaidAccount 149
LoggedIn 150
on computer 149
iCloud hack
URL 141
iCloud service 139, 140

iCloud storage
and backup overview, URL 173
idb
/etc/hosts file editor 168
about 165-169
Background screenshot 167
Certification manager 167
URL 187
iDevice
backup, on iCloud 140, 141
search and seizure 56
iDevice backup acquisition
about 141
and EPPB, with authentication
token 145-147
and EPPB, with username and
password 141-144
and iLoot, with username and
password 148, 149
iDevice backup analyzer 182
iDevice browsing tools 182
iDevice encrypted backup 183
iDevice, forensic community
advanced logical technique 57
backup or logical acquisition technique 57
direct technique 57
physical technique 57
iDevice identification 32-34
ideviceinfo command 33
iDevice operation, modes
Device Firmware Upgrade (DFU) 50
Normal 50
Recovery 50
iExplorer
about 58
URL 182
iFunBox
about 58
URL 182
iLoot
and iDevice backup acquisition, with
username and password 148
images
URL 95
iMazing
about 58
URL 182

IMEI.info
  URL 31
iMessage 98
Info.plist file 123
**Integrated Circuit Card Identification
    (ICCID) 18**
**International Mobile Subscriber Identity
    (IMSI) 18**
**International Organization of Computer
    Evidence (IOCE) 10**
Internet Evidence Finder
  URL 186
iOS 8 189
iOS analysis
  with Oxygen Forensics Suite 2014 112-116
iOS analysis suite 186
iOS Application Forensics
  URL 176
iOS apps, native
  about 91
  address book 91
  audio recordings 91
  calendar application 92
  call history 93, 94
  e-mail 94, 95
  images 95
  iMessage 98
  maps 96
  notes 96
  Safari 97, 98
  SMS 98
  voicemail 98
iOS backups (iTunes)
  restoring, URL 173
iOS configuration files
  about 89
  Account and device information 89
  Account information 89
  Airplane Mode 89
  Application installed list 90
  AppStore settings 90
  Configuration information and settings 90
  Lockdown certificate info 90
  Network information 90
  Notification log 90
  Passwords 90
  SIM card info 90

Springboard 90
System Logs 90
Wi-Fi networks 90
iOS data security
  about 50
  file, data protection 51, 52
  hardware security features 50
iOS device acquisition
  about 57
  advanced logical acquisition 66
  backup or logical acquisition 59
  direct acquisition 58
iOS device jailbreaking
  about 75
  with Elcomsoft iOS Forensic Toolkit 76-78
iOS devices
  about 23
  backing up, URL 173
  iDevice identification 32, 33
  iOS devices matrix 30
  iOS file system 34-36
  iOS operating system 31, 32
  iPad 27
  iPhone 23
  iPod touch 29
  restoring, URL 173
  security, URL 173
  URL 116
iOS devices matrix 30
iOS file system
  about 34
  data partition 42, 43
  device partition 40
  HFS+ file system 35-40
  property list file 44
  SQLite database 45
  system partition 41, 42
iOS forensics
  about 99
  clipboard 99
  Keyboard 99, 100
  location 100, 101
  snapshots 101
  Spotlight 102
  wallpaper 102
iOS Hardening Configuration Guide
  URL 175

iOS kernel 49
iOS Models
  URL 30
iOS operating system
  about 31
  Cocoa touch 31
  Core OS 31
  Core services 31
  Media 31
iOS Reverse Engineering Toolkit. *See* iRET
iOS Security
  URL 173
iOS Support Matrix
  URL 31
iOS Tracker
  URL 187
iPad
  about 27
  iPad 2 27
  iPad 3 (the new iPad) 28
  iPad 4 (with Retina display) 28
  iPad Air 28
  iPad (first model) 27
  iPad mini 28
  iPad mini second generation 29
  iPad mini third generation 29
  URL 31
iPad Tech Specs
  URL 173
iPad User Guide
  URL 173
iPBA
  iTunes backup analysis 127-130
IPBOX
  URL 191
iPhone
  about 23
  iPhone 3G 24
  iPhone 3GS 24
  iPhone 4 25
  iPhone 4s 25
  iPhone 5 25
  iPhone 5c 26
  iPhone 5S 26
  iPhone 6 26
  iPhone 6 Plus 26
  iPhone (first model) 24

jailbreaking 153-155
  URL 31
iPhone 4s
  UDID calculation 53, 54
iPhone Analyzer
  URL 183
iPhone Backup Analyzer
  URL 183
iPhone Backup Browser
  URL 183
iPhone Backup Extractor
  URL 183
iPhone Backup Unlocker
  URL 183
iPhone Backup Viewer
  URL 183
iPhone data protection tools
  URL 181
iPhone Data Recovery
  URL 184
iPhone History Parser
  URL 186
iPhone IMEI
  URL 31
iPhoneox
  URL 31
iPhone Tech Specs
  URL 173
iPhone Tools
  URL 186
iPhone Tracker
  URL 187
iPhone User Guide
  URL 173
iPod touch
  about 29
  iPod touch (fifth generation) 30
  iPod touch (first model) 29
  iPod touch (fourth generation) 30
  iPod touch (second generation) 30
  iPod touch (third generation) 30
  tech specs, URL 173
  URL 31
  user guide, URL 173
iRET
  about 162, 163
  Binary analysis 164

Database analysis 164
Header files 164
Keychain analysis 164
Log viewer 164
Plist viewer 164
Screenshot 164
Theos 164
URL 187
iSkysoft iPhone Data Recovery
URL 182
iStalkr
URL 187
iThmb Converter
URL 186
iTunes
URL 182
iTunes backup
about 119
analysis, with iPBA 127-130
content 120-122
data, extracting 127
encrypted iTunes backup, cracking 130
files, standard 123-125
folders 120
iTunes encrypted backup, cracking 130
iTunes encrypted backup cracking,
    with EPPB 131-135
structure 122
structure, URL 126
URL 120
with logical acquisition 59
iTunes Backup Extractor
URL 183
iTunes backup, files
Info.plist 123
Manifest.mbdb file 124, 125
Manifest.plist file 124
Status.plist file 124
iTunes encrypted backup cracking
about 130
with EPPB 131-135
iTunes Password Decryptor
URL 142
iXAM forensics
URL 181

J

jailbreaking tools
for iOS 6 184
for iOS 7 184
for iOS 8 184
URL 75
jailbroken devices 189

K

keyboard 99, 100
Keychain Dumper
about 157
URL 156

L

Lantern
URL 181
Law Enforcement
URL 173
Libimobiledevice
URL 182
location 101
location gate 100
lockdown certificate
about 55, 56
folders 55
lockdown certificates
folders 55
logical acquisition
advanced logical acquisition 66
with forensic tools 60
with iTunes backup 59
with Oxygen Forensic® Suite 61-65
with UFED Physical Analyzer 66-68
Low Level Bootloader (LLB) 49

M

Manifest.mbdb file
about 124
App domain 126
a. time 125
Camera Roll domain 126
c. time 125
domain 124

file hash 125
file size 125
Home domain 126
Keychain domain 126
link target 124
Managed Preferences domain 126
Media domain 126
m. time 125
path 124
Root domain 126
System Preferences domain 126
unix file permissions 125
user ID and group ID 125
Wireless domain 126
Manifest.plist file 124
manuals
  URL 172
maps 96
Master File (MF) 19
Mbdb file parser
  URL 183
MBDB format
  URL 175
MBDX format
  URL 175
memscan
  URL 159
message digest 17
MFC BOX
  URL 191
mobile device
  Airplane mode 13
  Faraday's bag 13
  jamming 13
  SIM card, removing 14
  switching off 13
Mobiledit Forensic
  URL 182
mobile forensics 8, 9
MobileTerminal tool 154

N

network service providers (NSP) 21
non forensic tools 182
non-jailbroken devices 190
notes 96

O

OpenSSH 154
Oxygen Forensics Plist Viewer
  URL 186
Oxygen Forensics SQLite Viewer
  URL 186
Oxygen Forensics Suite 2014
  iOS analysis with 112-116
Oxygen Forensics Suite Standard/Analyst
  URL 182
Oxygen Forensic® Suite
  logical acquisition with 61-65

P

P0sixspwn
  URL 184
Pangu
  URL 75
Paraben's Device Seizure
  URL 181
passcode
  URL 173
Passware Kit Forensics 65
PhoneView
  URL 182
physical acquisition
  with Elcomsoft iOS Forensic Toolkit 76-78
  with forensic tools 69, 70
  with UFED Physical Analyzer 70-75
physical acquisition tools 181
PIN unblocking key (PUK) code 12
Pip
  URL 186
plist Editor
  for Windows, URL 44
PlistEdit Pro
  URL 186
Plist viewer tools 186
PLOG block (Effaceable Storage) 50
property list file 44, 89
publications
  for free, URL 171, 172

R

readmem
  URL 159
Redsn0w
  URL 184
reports
  URL 172

S

Safari
  bookmarks 97
  cookies 97
  history 98
  screenshots 97
  search cache 97
  search history 98
  suspended state 98
  thumbnails 98
  web cache 98
Safari Forensic Tools
  URL 186
Santoku
  URL 33
search and seizure, iDevice 56, 79
SIM cards
  about 18-20
  security 21
  URL 14
Skype 102-104
SkypeExtractor
  URL 186
SkypeLogView
  URL 186
SMS 98
Smsiphone.org
  URL 183
Sn0wbreeze
  URL 184
snapshots 101
Spotlight 102
SpringBoard 32
SQLite
  deleted records, carving 112
  URL 89

database 45
SQLite Database Browser
  URL 45, 185
SQLite Expert
  URL 45, 185
SQLite Forensic Reporter
  URL 185
SQLite Manager
  URL 185
SQLite record carver 185
SQLite Recovery
  URL 186
SQLite Recovery Python Parser
  URL 185
SQLite Spy
  URL 185
SQLite Studio
  URL 185
SQLite viewer 185
Standard Working Group on Digital
    Evidence (SWGDE) 9
Status.plist file 124
Subscriber Identity Module (SIM)
    package 12
Super Crazy Awesome iPhone Backup
    Extractor
  URL 183
system partition
  about 41, 42
  URL 41

T

Taig
  URL 75, 184
third-party application analysis
  about 102
  Cloud storage applications 108
  Facebook 107, 108
  Skype 102-104
  WhatsApp 105, 106
timestamps 88
tools
  URL 172

U

UFED Physical Analyzer
  advanced logical acquisition with 66-68
  physical acquisition with 70-74
  URL 181
UFED Physical Analyzer/UFED 4PC/Ufed Touch
  URL 182
Ultra File Opener
  URL 187
Undark
  URL 186
unique device identifier 52
Unique Device ID (UDID)
  about 52
  calculation, on iPhone 4s 52-54
  URL 52
unique ID (UID) 50
Universally Unique ID (UUID) 86

V

voicemail 98
volume header file, fields
  allocationFile 38
  attributes 37
  attributesFile 38
  backupDate 37
  blockSize 37
  catalogFile 38
  checkedDate 37
  createDate 37
  dataClumpSize 37
  encondingsBitmap 38
  extentsFile 38
  fileCount 37
  finderInfo 38
  folderCount 37

  freeBlocks 37
  journalInfoBlock 37
  lastMountedVersion 37
  modifyDate 37
  nextAllocation 37
  nextCatalogID 38
  rsrcClumpSize 37
  signature 37
  startupFile 38
  totalBlocks 37
  version 37
  writeCount 38

W

wallpaper 102
Waterboard 66
WebBrowserPassView
  URL 142
WhatsApp 105-107
WinHex
  URL 185
Wondershare Dr.Fone iOS
  URL 182

X

XCode development platform
  URL 44
XRY
  URL 181, 182
X-Ways Forensics
  URL 185

Z

Zdziarski
  blog, URL 190-192
  URL 181

Thank you for buying
Learning iOS Forensics

About Packt Publishing

Packt, pronounced 'packed', published its first book, *Mastering phpMyAdmin for Effective MySQL Management*, in April 2004, and subsequently continued to specialize in publishing highly focused books on specific technologies and solutions.

Our books and publications share the experiences of your fellow IT professionals in adapting and customizing today's systems, applications, and frameworks. Our solution-based books give you the knowledge and power to customize the software and technologies you're using to get the job done. Packt books are more specific and less general than the IT books you have seen in the past. Our unique business model allows us to bring you more focused information, giving you more of what you need to know, and less of what you don't.

Packt is a modern yet unique publishing company that focuses on producing quality, cutting-edge books for communities of developers, administrators, and newbies alike. For more information, please visit our website at www.packtpub.com.

About Packt Open Source

In 2010, Packt launched two new brands, Packt Open Source and Packt Enterprise, in order to continue its focus on specialization. This book is part of the Packt Open Source brand, home to books published on software built around open source licenses, and offering information to anybody from advanced developers to budding web designers. The Open Source brand also runs Packt's Open Source Royalty Scheme, by which Packt gives a royalty to each open source project about whose software a book is sold.

Writing for Packt

We welcome all inquiries from people who are interested in authoring. Book proposals should be sent to author@packtpub.com. If your book idea is still at an early stage and you would like to discuss it first before writing a formal book proposal, then please contact us; one of our commissioning editors will get in touch with you.

We're not just looking for published authors; if you have strong technical skills but no writing experience, our experienced editors can help you develop a writing career, or simply get some additional reward for your expertise.

Practical Mobile Forensics

ISBN: 978-1-78328-831-1   Paperback: 328 pages

Dive into mobile forensics on iOS, Android, Windows, and BlackBerry devices with this action-packed, practical guide

1. Clear and concise explanations for forensic examinations of mobile devices.

2. Master the art of extracting data, recovering deleted data, bypassing screen locks, and much more.

3. The first and only guide covering practical mobile forensics on multiple platforms.

Computer Forensics with FTK

ISBN: 978-1-78355-902-2   Paperback: 110 pages

Enhance your computer forensics knowledge through illustrations, tips, tricks, and practical real-world scenarios

1. Receive step-by-step guidance on conducting computer investigations.

2. Explore the functionality of FTK Imager and learn to use its features effectively.

3. Conduct increasingly challenging and more applicable digital investigations for generating effective evidence using the FTK platform.

Please check **www.PacktPub.com** for information on our titles

Untangle Network Security

ISBN: 978-1-84951-772-0   Paperback: 368 pages

Secure your network against threats and vulnerabilities using the unparalleled Untangle NGFW

1. Learn how to install, deploy, and configure Untangle NG Firewall.

2. Understand network security fundamentals and how to protect your network using Untangle NG Firewall.

3. Step-by-step tutorial supported by many examples and screenshots.

Learning Pentesting for Android Devices

ISBN: 978-1-78328-898-4   Paperback: 154 pages

A practical guide to learning penetration testing for Android devices and applications

1. Explore the security vulnerabilities in Android applications and exploit them.

2. Venture into the world of Android forensics and get control of devices using exploits.

3. Hands-on approach covers security vulnerabilities in Android using methods such as Traffic Analysis, SQLite vulnerabilities, and Content Providers Leakage.

Please check **www.PacktPub.com** for information on our titles

Made in the USA
San Bernardino, CA
27 December 2015